AN AMERICAN STORY

AN AMERICAN STORY

EVERYONE'S INVITED

WILMER
VALDERRAMA

Harper Select

Published by Harper Select, an imprint of HarperCollins Focus LLC.

Published in association with United Talent Agency, LLC, 888 Seventh Avenue, 9th Floor, New York, NY, 10106, Attn: Albert Lee and Pilar Queen.

ISBN 978-1-4003-3659-3 (audiobook)
ISBN 978-1-4003-3658-6 (ePub)

Library of Congress Cataloging-in-Publication Data on File

ISBN 978-1-4003-3657-9

Printed in the United States of America

24 25 26 27 28 LBC 5 4 3 2 1

I dedicate this book to every person dreaming of a better life.

*To every parent who's sacrificed greatly so
your children can live their dreams.*

*To my mom and dad, mi mamá y papa, thank you for
showing me the path and for allowing me to walk it.*

*To my sisters, I wouldn't have a high school diploma if it
weren't for you. LOL. You know exactly what I mean.*

*To Amanda, for making us a home filled with love. And to Nakano,
I promise you that in your lifetime you will wake up one day
and the color of your skin will not be exotic; it will be your gift.*

To my nephew, Christian. You take it from here.

*To Tadao, my best friend, you know how I feel about you. But
in case you forgot, I love you, bro. Don't make it weird.*

CONTENTS

PROLOGUE

Present day

M y father is having a heart attack.

We're in his minivan, hurtling down the 405 freeway toward the hospital. I'm behind the wheel, and Dad's in the passenger seat next to me. He's clutching his chest, moaning softly. I'm trying to keep him as calm as possible. I want him alert and breathing. But he's fading in and out.

The traffic ahead of us has come to a stop. All I can see is a wall of brake lights. The freeway is as gridlocked as only Los Angeles can deliver. Even on a Sunday. But I can't be stopped. I veer to the side and drive on the shoulder, inches away from the tall graffitied cement barrier. I'm still speeding, whizzing by cars that aren't moving. My hazard lights are flashing, and my foot is pressed as hard on the accelerator as I dare. If I get stopped by the police, I'll ask for an escort.

"Dad," I say. "Which exit are we looking for?"

This is a ruse. I know exactly which exit we need. But Dad likes to give directions. My question is designed to keep him thinking, keep him talking.

Keep him alive.

To make matters worse, it's Father's Day.

Earlier that morning, Amanda and I had arranged for my father and my father-in-law, my nephew, me, and a few friends to go deep-sea fishing. It was a special gift. Out on the boat with the deep blue sea tossing us about, my father grew seasick. We gave him medicine for his nausea. But now, speeding toward the hospital, I suspect that the medicine has raised his heart rate, triggering the attack.

On land, after the fishing expedition was over, we'd all climbed into the car and started back to the house where my sisters had arranged a surprise dinner and Father's Day card game. Dad had napped a bit in the car, then woken up and said in Spanish, "My chest is really hurting." Plus, he couldn't feel his hand. He insisted on going to the house—no hospital. By the time we arrived, his chest had tightened like a vise. He'd broken out in a cold sweat and he felt lightheaded and dizzy. By then, I knew we were too late to call an ambulance. I strapped him into his minivan and put my foot to the floor.

"Dad," I say, still zooming past cars. "The hospital's right around here. You sure you know the right exit?"

"*Mijo . . .*" he says. His deep voice is ever familiar to me. But he doesn't finish his sentence. That is the only word he says. His favorite term of affection for me. He closes his eyes.

At the hospital, I speed into the emergency room drop-off area and screech to a stop. It's like we're in the movies, except this is nothing but real life.

"I need help!" I shout. "I'm losing my dad!"

Medical staff rush out, place him on a gurney, take him inside immediately. A man in a uniform tells me to go park the car and keep the area clear. When I return, I'm able to go inside. A staffer says, "Your father is having a major heart attack. But our cardiologist is out for the weekend. We're going to take your dad to another hospital." She tells me the address, and I punch it into my phone. Dad's already in an ambulance. I run back to the minivan and race to the second location.

This time a doctor meets me. "If you had gotten here fifteen minutes later, your dad wouldn't be around," he says. "We're prepping him for surgery right now."

They give me one minute with him. I say, "Dad, you're in good hands. All of us will be here when you get out. Just relax. I'll see you in a little bit." I take his hand in mine, kiss the top of his forehead. It's time for him to go. He looks at me with steady, unblinking eyes. They roll him away.

I take two steps back, turn around, stagger. Brace myself against a wall. The full weight of this moment has hit me. The words stream through my mind, *That may well have been the last time I see my father alive.*

And in a split second that's hard to describe, I remember the journey. I remember it all.

CHAPTER 1

Rising Up

1983

I t's early in the morning, at dawn's first light, when I pad into my parents' bedroom in Miami—where I was born—jump up onto the foot of their bed, a hairbrush microphone in hand, and start singing.

Loud.

At age three, I don't know English, and we speak only Spanish in the home, but I belt out a one-song concert using words I've memorized from the radio: "Eye of the Tiger" by Survivor. I do all my best dance moves, stepping and sliding on the bedspread like I have butter on the soles of my feet. When I finish, I bow and twirl an imaginary top hat, then fall laughing into my dad's outstretched arms.

"*Mijo,*" whispers my father into my ear with his deep, husky voice, holding me close and addressing me with the term of affection that Latino parents use for a beloved son. "*Naciste para entretener.*"

You were born to entertain.

"*Sí,*" adds my mother, one eye still closed. "But next time maybe later in the morning, eh?"

"You haven't heard my voices yet," I protest in Spanish. I break free from Dad, leap to my feet again, clasp an invisible cigarette in one hand, and scat my best Vegas Rat Pack tune, just like Sammy Davis Jr. Dad chuckles harder this time, and even Mom cracks a grin. I follow up with a perfect Elvis, sneering my upper lip and shimmying my knees while singing "Hound Dog."

Even at this early age, I've closely watched specials on TV, intently studying each guest, and I've perfected plenty more voices: Sylvester Stallone, Mr. T, El Puma (a big Latin pop star), Oscar D'León (a big salsa singer), Juan Gabriel (a Mexican icon), Kermit the Frog and half a dozen other Muppets—anything to make my parents laugh, even mimicking the sounds of our neighbor's dogs if it gets a chuckle. I rip through my voice repertoire one by one.

My little sister, Marilyn, toddles into the room, rubbing her eyes, her hair a wonderful mess of morning tangles. I was born on January 30, 1980, and she was born just over a year later, in February 1981. Already she is my best friend. She hums the last few bars of "It's Not Easy Being Green" with me, Kermit's favorite song, and starts to laugh.

We have so much potential at the start. Our whole family does. The future stretches wide before us, and we can do anything. Be anything. We have an intense love for each other and strong spirits. And we have big dreams.

Like all dreamers, all we need now is big opportunity.

WE LIVED IN A SMALL HOUSE IN MAGIC CITY THEN— the fitting nickname for Miami—where Dad had met, fallen in love with, and married Mom when they were barely adults. Dad had come to Miami from Venezuela originally, and Mom from Colombia. Our family wasn't poor when I was little, at least not that I remember. It always seemed like we had plenty, including a house with a tidy front yard and even a pool out back where Marilyn and I splashed in the constant Florida heat, Mom always nearby keeping a close watch on us.

My father, Balbino Valderrama, traveled most days, often working odd jobs or buying farm machinery in the United States and exporting it into Venezuela to rent out to farmers. When he came home from his trips, he sometimes had a faraway look in his eyes, as if he missed the land of his birth—or at least dreamed of what it might offer him now.

Evenings after dinner as I played with my G.I. Joe action figures in front of the TV, I'd hear bits and pieces of conversation between my parents. I didn't understand everything about what they were saying, but often they talked in hushed and excited voices. Dad more so than Mom. The economy of Venezuela in the early 1980s was racing upward, beginning to soar. The oil crises of 1973 and 1979 were over, and Venezuela was fast becoming the third-largest oil-producing nation in the world. Dad wasn't interested in a career in oil, but wealth was flowing, and Dad's dream was to have his own land in his home country so he could work his own farm.

I knew he'd had it rough in the past. Dad and his family were very poor. At age eight, he dropped out of school to care for his four brothers and two sisters. Jobs for eight-year-olds were scarce in Venezuela, and times grew so tough that Dad sometimes swiped sandwiches off the street so his siblings could eat. He never took food for himself. Only for his brothers and sisters. As the second oldest, he was the leader, already the man of the family.

Dad never met his real father. His alcoholic stepdad abused the family. His mother worked in a bakery all night, came home early each morning to care for her children as best she could, then slept a bit before her long day began again. Any money she brought home was grabbed by the stepdad and squandered on booze.

When my dad turned thirteen, the family agreed they'd taken

enough abuse. My father, still a sinewy teenager, packed a few meager possessions for the family and led his mother and siblings north to the city of Caracas. There, he hustled enough work to find his mother a little hut and settle the younger kids. For several years he worked in the slums and helped his mother get established in a job. By the time he was sixteen, the family was doing a bit better, so Dad started traveling on his own. He went to Paris, New York, Miami, always in search of a way he could earn more money to send home, always on a quest for a better life.

My mother, Sobeida Valderrama, was born in Colombia, one of the eldest of fourteen children. Her father owned a coffee farm where he cultivated and roasted his own beans. As a family they weren't wealthy, but they were rich in hard work, hope, and faith—and they never missed a Sunday Mass. After high school, Mom became a receptionist in a doctor's office in Colombia and started praying for the next open door. An older sister lived in Miami, and one summer Mom traveled to see her. There, she met my father. It was magic in the Magic City. Love at first sight.

When we kids came along, Dad adopted the role of family encourager, while Mom was the enforcer. Stern but loving, she taught us self-discipline and respect, although she never told me outright that she loved me—at least not with words. Growing up, she'd been taught to put herself last, so as an adult she had a tough time communicating love through words or kisses. Her way of showing love was to cook.

Mom fed me plate after plate of hot stuffed *arepas*, the staple of every Colombian and Venezuelan meal; it's like naan or pita bread, except made with corn flour. Each night she grilled beefsteak or pork, or she prepared deep-fried fish, showering the meat with fresh lime juice. Another favorite was *guasacaca*, an all-purpose guacamole dip blended with mayo and lime juice and spices. For snacks, she stuffed me with delicious *cachapas*, flavored fried corn dough, sometimes topped with butter and cheese. Meal after meal, I gorged myself on empanadas and crispy *tostones*—the golden brown twice-fried plantains that are pounded flat and covered in savory salt. A big pot of *sancocho* always bubbled on our stove. It's a traditional soup, more like a stew, with meat and vegetables, garlic, onions, potatoes, taro, and cilantro.

One day, still in Miami, Dad brought home for us a huge fluffy black dog, a chow chow breed, with a lolling purple tongue and a mass of hair. It looked like a baby bear, like no dog I'd ever seen.

"What do you want to name her?" Dad asked.

I blurted the first word that came to mind. "Negro." The color *black* in Spanish.

"I have another surprise for you and your sister," Dad said. "A trip to the toy store. For this time only, you can both get anything you want."

That wasn't like Dad to have two surprises for us so close together, but Marilyn and I jumped around in crazy excitement at the news. Dad drove us to the store, where my sister picked out a Barbie doll and I chose a Rancor—one of those hideous *Star Wars* reptile monsters with sharp fangs, long arms, and big claws.

Dad shook his head when I showed it to him. "No," he said. "Too ugly. Go put it back and get something else. Maybe a Mickey Mouse."

I stared deep into my dad's eyes. I was a respectful kid, but even at a young age I had a strong sense of self. I knew exactly what I wanted, and I would stand my ground. Dad didn't look like he was going to change his mind, so I went and put the Rancor back and returned empty-handed.

"Where's the toy?" Dad asked.

"I don't want anything except that." I stared deep into his eyes again, trying hard to communicate my seriousness.

For a moment he stared back at me, then let out a sigh of exasperation. "Fine," he said. "Go get your ugly-ass toy."

In that moment, I learned a lesson. It helped establish a character trait—determination—that would serve me well over the years to come. I wouldn't get angry. I wouldn't throw a fit. But neither would I change my passion for glory, just like the Survivor song said. I knew that if you have a specific dream, you can't settle for less. You get that eye of the tiger and pursue exactly what you want.

Dad had one more surprise for us that evening—this one bigger and more life interrupting than I could imagine. We went home, toys in hand, our dog, Negro, greeting us with slobbery hand licks when we walked through the front door. At the dinner table, Dad announced to us kids that next week we were moving. Mom already knew.

"Away from our home?" I asked.

"I have bought our family some land," he said with a loud *thump* on his chest. The determination in his eyes told me he also knew a thing or two about not settling for a lesser dream.

"But where?" I asked.

Dad grinned. "Venezuela."

OUR SHAGGY DOG MOVED TO VENEZUELA WITH US, when I was just three. Nobody in this new country had seen anything like him. One neighbor wasn't convinced that Negro was actually a dog. Who were these weird new people from the United States, and what kind of strange creature had they brought with them? Dad assured our neighbors that all was fine, and we were just like them, all hoping for big opportunity.

Our new farm lay about four hours south of Caracas, just outside the small town of Acarigua-Araure, Estado Portuguesa, right next to the tropical rainforest. Acarigua-Araure was actually two little towns pushed close together, so everyone referred to the area as one.

Dad bought a small house for us in town. He liked the idea of his family being close to shops and schools and cool little restaurants, so Dad planned to commute each day out to the farm to work. Our property in the country was just as much a ranch as a farm, and Dad proudly drove us out and showed us the lay of the land. We owned hundreds of acres—rich, fertile land as far as I could see in any direction. Dad planned to raise cattle and pigs, grow corn and rice, and harvest wood. Looking back, it was an ambitious plan, but I trusted my father. We were also going to have horses, and I would soon learn to ride, he promised. Maybe in a year or two. I couldn't believe my good fortune. I loved horses! And with a horse, I could become my favorite TV character.

To say that TV was already a big part of my life, even at that early age, was an understatement. Mom made sure we got plenty of fresh air outside too; it wasn't like Marilyn and I were couch potatoes. But TV fascinated me. In Miami, I'd watched as much as I could. In Acarigua-Araure, there were only two channels—Venevisión and Radio Caracas. The two channels played reruns of many of my favorite shows from the USA, all dubbed in Spanish. Once we were settled in our new house, I watched the same episodes again and again. *CHiPs* was a huge favorite, with all the motorcycles and action. The costar Erik Estrada, who played Ponch, was one of the few Latino actors on TV back then, and he became a childhood hero of mine. I loved *The Six Million Dollar Man*, *Charlie's Angels*, *The Incredible Hulk*, and *The Amazing Spider-Man*. We had Japanese cartoons that America didn't have, and I also watched Bugs Bunny and *The Tom and Jerry Show*.

But my favorite by far was the Walt Disney action-adventure Western series *Zorro*, starring Guy Williams. That's where my horse factored in.

My horse was black, just like Zorro's horse. I named him Tornado, just like Zorro's horse. Dad showed me how to brush Tornado, place a pad and a saddle on his back, and adjust and secure the straps. I learned how to place the reins over Tornado's head and guide his muzzle between the nose band and headstall, careful to place his ears in the gap between the crownpiece and browband.

Zorro, the TV show, was all about having adventures. He was educated and romantic and stood for the people. The show was set just outside Los Angeles in 1820, when the city was still part of Spanish California. Zorro solved mysteries and helped out good folks—all with heaping amounts of panache, and all while riding his horse.

Already he and I had a lot in common. Zorro could speak Spanish. So could I. Zorro rode a horse. So did I. He was heroic and gentlemanly and he fought for justice. That was exactly the kind of man I wanted to become someday.

Except my horse didn't come when I whistled like Zorro's did. I had to walk toward Tornado. *No problem,* I thought, *I'd figure that out soon.*

One afternoon while riding Tornado across the Venezuelan grassland, even at seven years old, I considered the implications of my name and my future. Wilmer Valderrama. To me, the name means "strong determination." It's a common name in Latin countries, and it connotes passion, drive, and a will to succeed. I dug my heels into Tornado, and together we galloped across the farmland. One day I would become someone just like Zorro, living big dreams, living with the same kind of integrity, doing noble things. I had no idea of how to get from here to there. But surely I was well on my way.

FIRST, I HAD TO LEARN HOW TO DRIVE A TRACTOR. I was eight when I first had the chance. Dad swung me up onto his lap on the tractor seat, ordered me to grasp the steering wheel with both hands, and started the big John Deere engine. Together, we rumbled out onto one of our fields.

Everything fascinated me about the tractor. The smell of the gasoline. The hard plastic feel of the steering wheel. The dusty windows from the day of work that Dad had already done. Now, as the evening sun set, he switched on the big overhead lights, and we drove a few laps with me steering and Dad shifting gears and calling out instructions. He was giving me a skill that might help me provide for a family one day. He was showing me how to become a true man.

Another thing I picked up from my dad was a healthy sense of pride. He never wore jeans and work boots, even when he labored in the field. Dad always wore a suit or polyester slacks, a dress shirt, and really nice shoes. Outside in the bright sun, he wore expensive Carrera sunglasses. He wore a gold chain around his neck and a gold ring on his pinky finger. Every morning he washed and blow-dried his hair, and his bronze face was clean-shaven except for a monster black mustache. He wore the look of a successful Latino businessman, and Dad dressed for success, even while driving the tractor, no matter how dirty he got. He soon had guys working for him on the farm. He always treated them well, and when he won, everybody else did too.

Mom looked elegant, too, but more understated. She liked to dress up if company came over, but most of the time she wore sandals, shorts, and a big T-shirt. We were doing well enough to have people help her around the house. Even then, Mom washed our clothes herself using one of those old-school washers with a tank and a basin. She hung our clothes out to dry on a clothesline. We were simple folks at heart. Most of the time, anyway.

One day Dad drove home in a brand-new Lincoln Continental—the most vivid color of burgundy I'd ever seen. He'd imported it from the United States, and ours was the only Lincoln in town. Dad had this way of building a beautiful energy around him. Whenever we went to restaurants with other families, Dad always picked up the check. If he saw friends at a table on the other side of the restaurant, he'd take care of their meal too.

Dad embodied bighearted giving. Certainly he was making up for the hard times he'd experienced as a child. But as an adult, he'd wanted to come back to Venezuela because the country still held out a promise to him. The work was here, a type of work that offered wealth. In the country of his birth, he could thrive at last. Now as a man, he was succeeding. I would mark this character trait of his and incorporate it into who I was becoming. Dad was a man who liked to work hard—and then give back.

We weren't much of a religious family, but we all believed in God. My mom was more spiritual than Dad probably, but we seldom went to church, except when I was little. Dad took me to my first Communion. I went into the confessional booth beforehand; thought hard about my deepest, darkest sins; then told them all to the priest. I didn't have much to confess, frankly, and I felt weird talking about all this stuff aloud. The priest told me to say a bunch of Hail Marys, but I wasn't comfortable with the whole arrangement, and when I came out of the booth, I asked my dad a sincere question: "What's to prevent me from committing the same sins this week, then coming back next week to confess them again?"

Dad smiled. "*Mijo*, I'm not going to make you go to church. But I am going to ask you to live by three principles. First, if you make a mistake and know it, then truly regret it. Own your own mistakes. Second, if you know you've made a mistake, then do something to fix it. Don't just let it lie. Third, it's okay to make mistakes. Everybody does. But when you know you've made a mistake and if you deliberately make that same mistake again, then you're failing yourself. You have to try with all your might not to make the same mistake twice.

That's how you become wiser. That's how you grow. Can you do those three things?"

I nodded. It seemed like a good way to live. Not perfectly. But wisely.

One evening, Dad swung me up onto his lap again. This time it was behind the wheel of his Continental. I hadn't turned eight yet. The steering wheel was soft and luxurious, not hard plastic like the John Deere, and I was paying more attention to the steering wheel than the road. The Continental drifted to the right and sideswiped a thornbush. We heard a loud scrape against the paint.

"Watch the road, Wilmer! Stay on course!" Dad yelled and grabbed me by my hair. Not hard enough to rip it. Just hard enough for me to know there are always consequences to actions. Quickly I steered the car back toward the center. Dad relaxed his grip.

Silently, I repeated his words so I wouldn't forget them. *Wilmer, stay on course.*

All of us have only select memories from our earliest years, but these are the types of memories that I carry with me to this day. For some reason, even at an early age, I would look for life lessons that I could use to guide me in my upcoming adventures.

WHEN I WASN'T RIDING MY HORSE OR WATCHING TV, I was going to the movie theater in our tiny town. There was only one theater in Acarigua-Araure, and it showed *RoboCop* year-round. *Part man, part machine, all cop.* I went so many times I nearly memorized the movie in English.

One of the most intriguing characters to me was Clarence Boddicker, the villain, portrayed by actor Kurtwood Smith. I didn't like the character's evil actions, but Kurtwood seemed to deliver each line with just the right amount of nasty enthusiasm. A true acting talent. I took mental notes on how he moved toward the camera, how he used his voice to play out a scene. I wondered if I could ever meet him someday. We could talk *RoboCop* all day long.

The plot of *RoboCop* centered on the city of Detroit in the near apocalyptic future. The city had collapsed financially and socially, and crime ran rampant. A private company was hired to do the police-work, and they tested this new prototype cyborg called RoboCop. I couldn't imagine a society ever collapsing so darkly. Certainly not ours. Everything in Venezuela was going well, at least according to what my father told us.

Meanwhile, I had kid stuff to do. I played baseball and soccer in a league in our town, and I applied myself in school and did well, for the most part. My worst grades were in English, a compulsory class in Venezuela. I couldn't imagine when I'd ever need it, so I didn't try hard to learn. I figured I knew enough English from memorizing *RoboCop.*

Studying the performing arts was also compulsory in Venezuelan schools, and my favorite classes were singing, dancing, and acting. When I sang, I felt like I was opening up, letting the light shine in. When I danced, I loved understanding how my body moved. When I acted, I could be outgoing and colorful. All three disciplines brought me much joy. Marilyn started kindergarten when I was in first grade, but she already knew how to read and write because she'd learned alongside me at home. She was so smart that school officials invited her to skip a grade. Soon enough, we were in the same class together, always best friends.

I was in my first school play at age seven. Our teacher taught us about symbolism and how in this particular play, a comedy, each of our characters represented certain noble character traits—or the opposite, certain vices. She stressed the importance of never breaking character. Once we were on that stage, anything could happen to distract us. A kid might forget his lines. An audience member might cough loudly. A true actor kept the play going—no matter what.

For weeks we rehearsed our play. On the big night, all the parents filed into the auditorium. The houselights dropped, and my heart began to pound like a jackhammer. I had only one line in this play, and I didn't want to blow it.

Just like Kurtwood Smith, I was the villain, one of the vices—and in this situation I represented temptation. I wore a little white suit with a box of cigarettes stuffed into the breast pocket, and in one hand I carried an empty whiskey bottle. When the time came for my big debut, I stumbled out onto center stage like I was drunk. One of my female schoolmates walked in front of me in a dress, and I slurred in Spanish the one line I'd carefully practiced: "Come over here, pretty lady, and say hello."

The audience exploded with laugher, just like they were supposed to, and at that exact second something jolted hard within me: a realization. I loved the instant feedback from the crowd, the energy of live action, the glow of the spotlight. With my line now uttered, I wanted to look around the darkened auditorium to study the crowd, try somehow to absorb this incredible energy emitting from them, replay this single moment of sheer exhilaration so I could live in this instant forever. But I stayed in character, gazing intently at the girl, waiting for the next line to come.

Suddenly the entire auditorium flooded with light. Some egghead backstage had brought up the houselights by mistake. This wasn't the right time! Out of the corner of my eye, I could see everybody in the audience—parents, teachers, students—staring at us, wondering what was going on. I was tempted to glance to stage right or stage left to see for myself. I wanted to shout at the stagehand to bring down the lights.

This play was going to flop—all because of his one mistake—with me right in the middle of it. But again my teacher's words flashed through my mind.

Never break character.

Without missing a beat, I swung my attention from the girl, looked at the audience, and raised my bottle in a toast. "*Salud*," I said, still pretending to be drunk, or maybe I just thought the word, and raising the bottle, was enough for the audience to catch my joke. They laughed again, even harder this time, and broke into applause, clapping, cheering, pounding their hands together. We were a hit. The play was a success.

Instead of freezing, I'd put it into gear. Instead of falling apart, I'd kept it going. Call it a moment of destiny. From that evening forward, all I wanted to do was be onstage.

WHEN I WAS EIGHT, MY PARENTS HAD ANOTHER daughter, Stephanie. She was a happy baby, filled with joy, and right from the start, we all loved her so much. But something dark was beginning to cloud my parents' lives, and Stephanie would never experience the richness of this land as we did, at least not to remember much of it. Our family had lived in Venezuela for five years by the time she was born, and Dad and Mom had started watching the news more intensely. Each night they talked in hushed tones again, but apart from the new baby, they weren't radiating much joy.

A year passed, and another year. I started watching the news with my parents. Each night came another report about soaring inflation, about another murder in the capital, about drugs and guns and gangs and violence. Dad muttered about how difficult it was becoming to make a decent living in this country. Farms the size of ours began struggling just to break even. Every time our tractor broke down, Dad needed to fly to Miami for parts. Everything was becoming more complicated.

I tried to make sense of what I was hearing, but it all seemed beyond me. Mostly, I tried to put the national conflict and fighting far away from my mind. I loved being in school plays and performed in as many as possible. I loved music recitals. Dance competitions. For each family member's birthday party, I did a solo act, telling jokes, singing songs, doing funny impersonations to entertain our guests.

The only fighting I ever did personally was in mixed martial arts class. I loved boxing, and early on I learned how to correctly throw a punch. It's funny: when you learn how to correctly throw a punch, you find yourself never in an actual fight where you need to throw one. I was confident I could take care of myself, so I learned how to laugh at playground insults.

I never had any enemies among my classmates. I was intense but easygoing. But if a kid talked crap about a family member of mine, I would see red. You could say anything about me personally, and I wouldn't care. But if you said something bad about a family member, that was considered a great insult in Venezuela. How was I supposed to know that in the United States, an entire pop subculture was built around telling "Yo Momma" jokes? Someday I'd learn. People could insult each other in a humorous way, and no one got mad.

I turned eleven, then twelve. One by one, Dad began to sell things that we owned. His wardrobe became more casual. He wasn't buying new shirts anymore. I'll never forget the day Dad sold his burgundy Continental. He still had his farm truck, but for everyday travels he bought a little moped.

A moped!

One night as Christmastime came closer, Mom put Stephanie to bed at her usual time, earlier than us bigger kids, and Dad gathered Marilyn and me together in the kitchen where he could speak to us privately.

"I'm sorry," he said. "We can't afford presents for you this year. Your mother and I need you to understand and have patience. We'll still get Stephanie a little something, but there's not enough money for you bigger kids."

I opened my mouth, alarmed, but Dad raised a finger to his lips for me to keep listening.

"We'll still have a Christmas celebration this year," he added. "Plenty of music, and a big meal. But what's underneath the tree won't be much."

I had the good sense to nod my understanding. I glanced at Marilyn. A fearful look crept into her eyes, and I put my hand on top of hers as a comfort. "It's okay," I said. "Mom and Dad know what they're doing. We'll be all right."

After that, I watched the news every night. It was difficult for a child to grasp exactly what was happening with Venezuela's politics in the early 1990s. I understood corruption. I grasped that promises were being broken and that political leaders had stopped talking to each other and refused to collaborate. Plenty of stories were about poverty. Inflation. Looting. Riots. People were becoming desperate. Venezuela was falling apart.

Early in the new year, a military officer named Hugo Chávez tried to seize control of the government. He'd been schooled in the philosophies of Marx and Lenin, and before his coup attempt, he'd made a lot of public promises to the people—more food, better housing, health care. He had his supporters. Chávez's first attempt at a coup failed, and he was thrown into prison. But almost overnight, mobs began demonstrating outside of Chávez's prison, demanding his release. The people who knew best saw this strong, frenzied support for Chávez and suspected the worst. Chávez wasn't the answer to our country's problems, but Chávez would be back.

Soon, our tractor was gone. Our farm truck was gone. Even Tornado was gone, which made me quite sad. At last, our entire farm was sold.

Not long after that, my dad sat us all down one evening and announced we were moving again. This time, back to the United States.

"We'll leave this Thursday," he said. "You'll need to learn English."

The only class I was failing!

The last item Dad sold was his humble moped. When Thursday came, a friend arrived in his car and drove us to the airport. We carried only our suitcases. Dad's entire life savings were tucked away in his pocket.

Our leaving wasn't a secret, and we didn't flee in the middle of the night or sneak past guards. Nothing like that. Venezuelans were still traveling to the United States regularly, and people knew that my parents had lived in Miami once, so our departure made sense to our neighbors.

But as my hometown grew smaller in the rearview mirror of our neighbor's car, I sensed it was a tense season for us as a family. For our whole country. Thanks to the grace of God, Dad had possessed the foresight to get us out early, when Venezuela still hadn't experienced her most troubling moments. But my aunts and cousins would not be so lucky. In time, they would also need to leave the country, but they would flee on foot, hungry and in rags, with the little they still owned being carried on their backs.

To slowly witness the collapse of Venezuela from the ground level, as I did in my childhood and early teenage years, felt like a great tragedy. It was the government's fault. Not the people's. The Venezuelan people are beautiful and vibrant, and to this day I hold my Venezuelan roots closely. With its vast reserves of oil, the Venezuela I knew was one of the most promising and richest countries in the world. Venezuela should have become the next Dubai.

Instead, it became a fractured wasteland. It failed to rise up.

We hoped the United States would give us a second chance.

CHAPTER 2

Fascinating and Petrifying

As the airplane touched down on American soil, I already knew this city was not our final destination. Dad made that clear from the start. Our family of five had taken off from Caracas three hours and fifteen minutes ago and headed to Miami only because the southeast corner of the United States was the cheapest place to land. Plus, Dad knew his way around Miami. This city would not be our home again, like it was a decade ago when I was three. We were headed for the West Coast—California—where Dad had relatives. Instead of driving there directly, Mom and Dad had a surprise planned.

We threaded our way through customs and headed to baggage claim, the airport a strange cacophony of sounds, restaurant aromas, and words I didn't recognize. Dad could speak and read a bit of the language. Just enough to get by. He led us to the rental car facility and filled out paperwork. The attendant handed him keys to a new sleek, white Ford Taurus station wagon.

"Hop in, kids," Dad said in Spanish. "Keep your eyes open."

My sisters and I grinned and spread out across the back seat. In the front, Mom settled in and stretched open the accordion folds of a paper road map—one of those enormous, impossible-to-close navigation aids that came from a service station—her brow furrowed. She studied the map for several minutes before saying to Dad, "*Interestatal 95. Norte.*"

North? We were going north! When would we ever get such a chance again? A real American road trip. My parents were handing us an opportunity to see our new country. I couldn't believe our luck. My mind raced, speculating on what we'd see. The American flag up close. Fun roadside attractions. License plates from famous states. Stuff we'd seen only in movies. Dad put the Taurus in gear and we headed out of Miami toward Jacksonville. First stop: a convenience store!

The three of us children stood transfixed in front of the snack section, mouths agape, staring at rows and rows of new snack foods. Dad told us to load up, anything we wanted to keep us quiet for the next three hundred miles.

Popcorn I recognized, and I knew I liked it. Chips were a favorite, although the brands in the United States were different. I puzzled over what looked like hunks of dark beef stuffed inside a sealed plastic bag. I couldn't read the labels, so I handed a package to Dad with raised eyebrows.

"*Carne seca,*" he said.

"Dried-up meat?" I asked. "Sure, I'll try anything. But first, what's that bright blue stuff over there?" I motioned to a counter where a large swirling machine sat with a spout near the bottom.

Dad just laughed.

Back in the station wagon, we kids surveyed our haul, and I tried my first-ever bite of beef jerky. Salty, smoky. Not as good as Mom's home cooking, but it definitely would become a new favorite. The beef jerky made me thirsty, so I washed it down with a long swig of the drink Dad had procured via the swirling machine. It tasted fruity, and I couldn't imagine what kind of wild American fruit might be blue, but

I didn't care. The drink was intensely sweet and slushy, like melting frost at the sides of our fields.

I took another long swig, twice as long as the first. Pain jolted through my head. My brain felt like it was squeezed in a vise. I let out a howl. This time, Mom just laughed.

STRANGE CARS WHIZZED PAST US ON THE FREEWAY. I knew my cars back in Venezuela. Small Toyota Hilux trucks were common, as were Fiats and Renaults. People held on to their cars for a long time in Venezuela. New cars, particularly in the last few years, were only a dream. In the United States, I saw the vehicles of affluence. Cadillacs. BMWs. Corvettes. Souped-up vintage Ford Gran Torinos, just like Starsky and Hutch drove. I spotted a strange car called a Mazda—what in the world was a Mazda?

We ate at Burger King for dinner. Another first. The flame-broiled cheeseburger tasted like the stuff of my dreams. That night at the motel, I couldn't believe how many channels we found on the TV. You could flip channels all evening and never watch a full show. In the morning, we splashed in the motel's pool, ate cereal with milk at the breakfast buffet, and hit the road again. We crossed the state line and headed into Georgia. I remembered from school that Martin Luther King Jr., the great American civil rights activist, had been born in Atlanta. He'd experienced much conflict in his short life while working to help all people become free. Black. Native Americans. Latinos, just like me.

Not long after lunch, Stephanie piped up from the back seat, letting us know she had to pee. Dad veered off at an exit and made a beeline for a gas station. Mom hustled Stephanie inside to the bathroom. Dad and Marilyn and I didn't need to go, so we stayed put. But right as Stephanie and Mom returned, Marilyn said she'd changed her mind. Dad looked at me and said, "You take her, *mijo*. Girls shouldn't walk alone."

"Inside, to the left," Mom added, fumbling with the map again. "Get the key from the man at the counter."

I gulped.

Marilyn and I climbed out of the rental car and walked toward the gas station. When I took her hand in mine, it felt strangely chilly, even though it was July in the Deep South. Back in Acarigua-Araure, it wasn't weird for a brother to take his sister's hand when they walked. Venezuela could be dangerous, violent. Holding hands showed folks that the girl was with a boy, protected, safe—nothing I felt at this moment. I wished Mom or Dad had come with us. This was my first time alone, needing to navigate this new culture as a kid. I knew there were a lot of Latinos in the United States. Yet left to fend for myself and my sister, I felt lost and scared.

The bell above the heavy glass door jingled as my sister and I walked in. I fixed my gaze downward at the floor until we were almost at the front counter. The clerk needed to finish ringing up a customer's order—a giant of a man dressed in work boots, blue jeans, and a white tank top. He wore a red bandana around his neck and was buying a six-pack of canned beer. The man turned to go, and the clerk glanced at me. My mind went blank. Even on the best of days, I didn't know how to ask for a bathroom or say *key* in English, so I just looked up at the clerk and tried to smile. He stared back at me and crossed his arms. A bead of perspiration slowly slid down my face. For a long moment, I didn't say anything, and neither did he. Then he muttered some words in English, gibberish to me. I motioned in the direction where Mom had said the bathroom was located. He glared at me again, then slowly reached under the counter, grabbed something, and plunked down a key in front of me.

"*Gracias*," I whispered.

Carefully I walked Marilyn toward the bathroom. The key worked. She went inside and shut the door. I stood outside, waiting, my eyes darting around the store. The man with the beer lingered near the magazine rack. Another guy studied oil cans near the far wall. A woman and two kids stood in the candy aisle, chattering among themselves. No one looked the same as me.

Please God, I said in my mind. *Please don't let anyone come up and talk to me. I don't know what to do. What if they ask me if someone's in the bathroom? I won't be able to tell them to wait.*

The moment mocked me. That's something I know today, many years later. A moment such as this can make even the most confident person feel fractured. Very few people understand how scary it is not to be able to speak English in the United States, particularly when you're a child with brown skin.

I heard a flush, then the sound of water running into a sink. Marilyn emerged, drying her hands on her jeans, her mouth firmly set in a straight line. I took the key back to the clerk, set it on the counter, and murmured "*Gracias*" again. Marilyn and I headed outside, and I took her hand in mine again on the long walk back to the car.

At least I had my sister. As we climbed into the back seat, I glanced in her direction, wondering if she'd sensed any of the same dread I did. Her skin looked pale, her mouth rigid, like she'd seen a ghost. I nodded.

She knew.

AS A WHOLE, AMERICA WAS BEAUTIFUL. STARING OUT the window as we drove, I felt like I had my very own movie screen to the scenery. We glimpsed the Great Smoky Mountains of Tennessee, amber waves of grain in Kentucky, and the Great Lakes Plains region of northern Indiana. Soon, we discovered the quintessential American family restaurant—Sizzler, where a mouthwatering steak could be had for a couple of bucks. That became our favorite dinner stop until Minneapolis, where we discovered Red Lobster, with its surf and turf on the menu. All-you-can-eat endless, battered, deep-fried shrimp. I mean, come on!

From Minnesota, we shifted directions and headed southwest toward Nevada. We stopped at roadside attractions and took snapshots. For hours, we listened to the radio—songs I hadn't heard at home. It felt like a vacation but different in one important way: when this trip was over, we wouldn't be returning to Venezuela. We would start from scratch and journey to a new life. The United States was our home now, and we had to figure it out.

Everywhere I looked, something seemed larger than life. In Las Vegas, we stayed at a hotel across the street from where a new hotel and casino called Treasure Island was being built. When we drove into our hotel's parking lot, we couldn't see much of anything from the street because big walls blocked our view. But upstairs in our room I could look down and see the construction site.

"Dad!" I yelled. "You'll never believe this. A huge pirate ship!"

To me, this was magical. Here was a huge ship right in the middle of the desert. Only in America. I was so wide-eyed by what I'd seen so far on this road trip, it made it difficult to miss what we'd left behind.

When we finally drove into Los Angeles, the city seemed to spread out forever. Palm trees dotted the sides of ten lanes of freeway, and far on the horizon I could see the skyline of downtown LA. We drove straight to my uncle's house in Van Nuys, parked at the curb, and climbed out. Dad's brother had invited us to stay with them for a couple of months until my father secured a job and found us a place of our own to rent.

My uncle emerged and gave us all hugs. His wife waved from the window. The cousins crowded around and said hello, but they spoke only English, so it was impossible for anyone to be understood. I'd met my uncle once back in Venezuela when I was young, but our families weren't close, and I hadn't met my aunt or cousins until now or even heard about them until recently.

Our relatives owned a house about the same size as the one we'd rented a decade ago in Miami. Their house had three small bedrooms. My aunt and uncle kept one room. My parents stayed in another; little Stephanie would sleep in their bed with them. The cousins doubled up and took the last bedroom. Marilyn and I slept on mattresses on the living room floor.

Everything felt crowded, and it was clearly their house, not ours. Their kitchen was tiny, and even though Mom promised to help with cooking and Dad said he'd help pay for groceries, I wasn't so sure how my aunt felt about the whole arrangement. She never seemed to smile around us.

Days passed, and Dad went to work temporarily at the rental car agency that my uncle ran. Mom helped out around the house. Whenever we watched TV with the cousins, we watched their favorite shows, not ours, and nothing was dubbed into Spanish like it'd been back home. Sometimes Marilyn and I went to the front yard and tossed a ball back and forth, but life seemed to have taken a sober turn. It was the start of August, the grand adventure of our road trip was over, and our new life in Los Angeles had begun.

Mostly, we killed time, waiting. For a house of our own. For a permanent job for Dad. I wondered what school would be like when it began in a couple of weeks. The days weren't all bad. I noticed that when the sun set in Los Angeles, the sky turned a stunning shade of pink, like nothing I'd seen before. Dad turned in the Taurus and borrowed one of my uncle's rental cars. On Saturdays, he took us to the beach in Santa Monica. We ate at a restaurant called Gladstones, where they served clam chowder inside bread bowls. Imagine that. Soup inside a loaf of bread. His car soon needed to be put back into rotation, so Dad shelled out some of his savings and bought a used car. The paint was faded and the seats were cracked from the sun, but it ran. It was one of those compact Mazdas that didn't exist in Venezuela, and for that reason alone, I thought our new car was supercool.

After two weeks, I noticed my aunt would fuss whenever we were nearby. Everybody tried their best, but clearly, we were in their space. Tension grew each day. My mother and my aunt weren't getting along in the kitchen, and sometimes at night I could hear my aunt and uncle talking in English behind the walls of their bedroom. I couldn't understand anything they were saying, but from the tone, I sensed a time bomb was ticking.

One hot afternoon toward the end of August, the Santa Ana winds were blowing like a hair dryer, and Marilyn and I were playing outside. We went into the kitchen to cool off, and I opened the freezer and pulled out a popsicle. My aunt stood nearby and gave a little start. She strode to me, ripped the popsicle from my hand, and threw it back in the freezer. "That's not for you," she hissed.

Mom was beside the fridge and witnessed the incident. Her fuse was low too. My aunt was physically the bigger person, but Mom glared at her and said, "You will *never* take food from my children again!" My aunt grimaced. Suddenly they were shoving each other, pulling each other's hair. Everything blew up. We kids watched, frozen, until one of the cousins jumped on the phone, and my dad and uncle rushed home to break up the fight.

That was it. They told us to leave. We packed up our stuff with speed, climbed into our Mazda, and took off. Dad drove us to a cheap motel nearby, all he could find. I looked around at the peeling paint, tacky wallpaper, two queen beds, and realized the truth: we were in a hard place. The careful plans my parents had created to ease us into our new life had backfired. We were in this country without a safety net.

The motel had no kitchen, so we started eating out each night. That took money. Dad's job at the rental car company was gone now, so day after day he hit the pavement, searching for work. He tried to find us a place to rent, but he had no credit history in the United States and no employment. More than once, Marilyn edged up to me and asked, "Are you sure we're going to be okay?"

Finally Dad pieced together a job delivering parts for auto stores. His hours were long, and it wasn't much money, but it was a beginning. Every day he worked his ass off, but no place would rent to us, which meant we were stuck at the motel, still eating out every night, burning through my parents' meager savings. At last, with his new job, just before the start of school, he persuaded a landlord to rent us a tiny house. Two bedrooms. Mom and Dad took one; the girls and I all piled into the other. At least it was better than the motel.

And then came school.

MOM AND DAD ENROLLED MARILYN AND ME AT Mulholland Middle School. A few days before classes started, our parents took us to the school building and came inside with us while Dad talked to the administrators in his broken English, explaining who we were and that we didn't speak English.

I was supposed to be in seventh grade. But they put me back in sixth because of my inability to speak English. Marilyn was also set back a year, so she landed in sixth along with me. This was the grade she would have been in originally, because she'd skipped a grade back in Venezuela.

A day or so later, school began. Dad dropped us off at the curb, and we were on our own. Thank God I had my sister. That first morning, we clutched hands and waded into the vast sea of junior high students, all bubblegum-popping strangers, and carefully eased our way inside the main building. We didn't know how to find our classrooms. We couldn't read our schedules. We couldn't make sense of our textbooks. We couldn't write reports in English, or understand questions and take tests, or even ask anyone for help.

Somehow, we figured out the day started with something called "homeroom." It took a few tries, but we finally found the right classroom. The teacher said something to us when we walked inside, which I guessed was a greeting and an order to sit. A bell rang, and she started saying what I gathered was each student's name. I began to sweat. Each kid answered with the same strange word—something that started with a *p*. I couldn't make out the word—either to understand what it meant or even to mimic its sound when it came time for me to speak. I glanced at Marilyn. Her eyes were wide and she was trembling. She looked back at me, but all I could offer was a stiff shrug. Thank God our last name is Valderrama.

All the rest of that morning sucked. A science teacher scribbled what looked like three days' worth of lessons on the chalkboard. I didn't understand a word. A language arts teacher passed out copies of a novel I guessed we were supposed to read, but when I opened my book, I couldn't grasp a thing. Marilyn and I had every class together, fortunately, and at lunchtime, we sat by ourselves and tried to avoid eye contact with everybody. The other kids ignored us. Everybody already had their own circle of friends. My sister and I picked at our sandwiches, too dazed and confused to eat.

Near the end of that first day, we went to a class called "ESL": English as a Second Language. Every kid in that room looked as petrified as we felt. A few spoke Spanish, but plenty of other languages were being spoken too. We were all mixed up together. I picked up a few words and tried to remember them, but when class was over and the next day began, I couldn't recognize any words that we'd learned when kids and teachers actually spoke. It's one thing to learn English formally inside a classroom, but when people speak English in real life, they talk so crazy fast you have no idea what's being said.

I quickly learned that English is an incredibly complicated language. Rules of grammar are loose and few, and just when you think you've learned something, you discover a variant. That rule about "*i* before *e* except after *c*" is a load of shit. It doesn't matter how those two vowels are placed together anyway, they never sound the same. There's *seize* but *glacier. Height* but *weight.* I mean, make up your mind, English. And consider those confounding *ous. Though. Through. Thought. Tough. Thorough. Trough.* What a puzzle. If you grow up speaking English, you might not realize how singsong the language can be. Your *ADDress* is where you live. But when you *addRESS* somebody, you speak directly to them. Contractions consistently baffled me. "I didn't" sounded so different than "I did not," particularly when somebody spoke quickly. The words *subtle, Wednesday, rhino,* and *solemn* have more letters than sounds, and why in the hell would you ever begin *knead* with a *k? Jeep* rhymes with *beep,* but *jeer* rhymes with *beer,* and you can't even count on the *ed* at the end of a word to sound the same. There's *marched* but *printed, developed* but *barred.* Even after a couple months of ESL, my verbs were all over the place, and I was forever using the wrong tense. *Tomorrow, I had been going to the store.* In English, there are something like twelve tenses just for the single verb *to be.* After you learn all those, you've got buckets of other verbs and their tenses to master. *I have. I see. I give. I run. I swim. I work. I ignore. I barf.* You have compound verbs. Irregular verbs. Linking verbs. Haystacks of verbs. Kids would look at me and shake their heads. Or laugh. Nobody had any idea what I was saying. Plus, all that 1990s slang that kids spoke in the hallways was an entirely different language than the one we were learning in ESL. *Booyah. As if. My bad. Totally bugging. Gettin' jiggy.* Some kid barked at another kid to "take a chill pill." A teacher looked at me when I walked into the classroom and said "'Sup?" I was like, "What the *what*?"

Mostly, I chose not to communicate. If I kept my mouth shut, I might stay safe. Day after day was difficult. Whenever Marilyn and I came home from school and Mom asked us how our day had been, neither of us wanted to talk about it. It was always the same. One hard day after another. We turned on the TV at home to keep learning English. TV helped and we watched a lot, but even that can feel like overload. After a whole day of not understanding, sometimes you don't want any more.

That whole first school year sucked. There's no nice way of saying it. Day after day. Week after week. Month after month. I lived in fear. School was the worst.

SLOWLY, VERY SLOWLY, A FEW THINGS BEGAN TO HELP. We made friends with some kids in the ESL classes. It's hard to build community when you're all living in fear, but after a while, Marilyn and I started hanging out with a few kids at lunchtime, not just each other.

And I got back into acting. My first play at Mulholland was *Beauty and the Beast* in the spring of my sixth-grade year. I'd just turned thirteen. I couldn't say the lines in English, so I wore the costume for the Beast onstage and did all the moves and blocking, while offstage the teacher shouted my lines for me. When the Beast turned into the prince, a different kid played him. Theater felt familiar, and I finally was having a bit of fun in school.

That same spring, my dad enrolled me in the San Fernando soccer league, and I made a few friends there, mostly Latino kids. Being outside moving around was better than being stuck inside a classroom all day. Still, nothing came easy. I had to figure out the coach's instructions.

You'd think you could learn English in six months, maybe a year, depending on your age, how hard you worked at it, and how immersed you are. But experts say it can take a few years before you're truly fluent. Even longer if you're trying to master all the nuances of the language. By the time I started seventh grade, I had a smattering of English, but I was far from conversant. I did a few more plays, and I started getting parts with dialogue. The more plays I did, the more I started to digest the language.

At the start of seventh grade, an eighth grader named Ryan Tomilson must have noticed I was having trouble fitting in, because simply from a place of generous humanity, I think, he started saying hi to me each morning. Ryan was a year ahead of me in school and a popular kid, into skateboarding and surfing, and he played in a band. At first, I would just nod. I was still so scared to talk to anyone. But Ryan kept at it. We didn't have any classes together, and we were never best buds, but whenever he saw me in the hallways or cafeteria, he simply said hello. Ryan knew a couple of Spanish words and phrases, so sometimes he'd try some of his Spanish out on me at lunchtime. Once in a while, he even invited Marilyn and me to sit at his lunch table.

Ryan was the first white kid who went out of his way to befriend me. His actions were pretty simple. But thanks to him, I actually started looking forward to coming to school. I knew that one person was going to say hello to me, and that straightforward, daily interaction helped me feel like I slightly belonged. I wasn't in school with a bunch of complete strangers anymore.

As immersed in English as Marilyn and I were at school, we were still highly immersed in Spanish at home, other than the English we heard on TV. Dad could speak just enough English to get by, but Mom didn't learn English for years. We always spoke Spanish in our house, and even to this day, I still communicate in Spanish with my parents. My mother started learning English in earnest a few years ago.

Nowadays I invite people to put themselves in her shoes. Sometimes English-speaking Americans hear stories like hers and get upset. They'll say (or think) things like, "Look, if you want to come to this country, you need to learn English." Which looks good on paper or in politics. But really, that mindset doesn't fully grasp the issues that people who don't speak English encounter when they move to the United States. If you don't learn English, people think you're lazy or resistant to your new culture. But that's not correct.

Picture my mother. She's a smart, capable woman, with more energy than three people put together. Her husband was working up to fourteen hours a day at his new job, trying to earn enough to put food on the table and a roof over our heads. She was tasked with managing the household. Mom still had a five-year-old at home. Every day, Mom made sure Marilyn and I were up in the morning, dressed, fed, and off to school. She cared for Stephanie during the day, while she cooked and swept floors and did laundry and took care of errands. When Marilyn and I came home after school, Mom helped with our homework and made sure the family was fed dinner, and that Stephanie was bathed, and that lunches were ready for the next day. Anytime she went to a store, Mom needed to figure out a new system. Try planning a shopping list or a weekly menu when only a few of the ingredients you're familiar with are stocked at the store. Try taking a sick child to the doctor when you need to navigate a new culture. Try meeting with your child's teacher if they're having trouble in a school subject. Try going to the bank. Try shopping for car insurance. Try buying stamps or mailing a package at the post office.

Mom had left behind all her friends in Venezuela. Those were the days before Skype or FaceTime or Zoom. Email was brand new, and few people had it. Making a long-distance call cost big money, which our family didn't have. You could still write a letter, but that took time. Mom was lonely. It was hard to make new friends. In all the years we kids were in school, Mom consistently put herself last. It's hard enough being a parent when everything's going well. Those years were really rough on her.

I've seen plenty of hardworking immigrants who have been in America for ten, twelve years who still don't know how to speak English. And believe me, it's easier said than done. It's hard to learn the language when you're overwhelmed, trying to keep your family afloat. Many immigrants are just trying to survive. People will insist, "Speak English. You're in America." That drives me crazy. Mine is a frustration born from experience. And I think we all need to have some patience. We have to realize that this country was settled by immigrants, and unless you're Native American, every person or their grandfather was new to this country once. Today I like to say, "America, let's be more hospitable." We need to be more respectful to our guests.

DAD FIGURED OUT A SIDE BUSINESS FLIPPING CARS. OUR Mazda was soon gone, sold at a tiny profit, and Dad bought a slightly better car. He immediately put a "For Sale" sign in the window and advertised it as he drove his delivery routes between auto parts stores. Soon that car was sold, and he bought another Mazda, better than the first. I wondered if he was trying to work his way up to another

Lincoln Continental, but I never asked. In Venezuela, he'd been a wealthy businessman. When he came to the United States, he had to start from scratch.

One night in our tiny, rented duplex in Los Angeles, about eleven o'clock, I was asleep in the bedroom I shared with my two sisters. I heard a commotion in the living room and opened my eyes. Carefully, I slid from under the covers and padded out to where my parents were talking loudly. The stark overhead lights in the living room blazed full and cold, and I quickly realized that the commotion wasn't because they were having an argument. They were frantic. My mother was sobbing. Her whole body contorted in a tight clench. Dad was wringing his hands, staring at the floor.

"*¿Cuál es el problema?*" I asked, alarmed. I was instantly wide awake.

"Our car," my father muttered in Spanish. He shook his head. "Stolen."

I glanced from my mother to my father. I had never seen such fear in my parents' eyes. It was clear that no one knew what to do. This car was our lifeline. That old clunker of a Mazda was all that was keeping us afloat. It had been stolen from where Dad left it, parked in front of our duplex. If Dad didn't have a car, he would lose his job. My parents' savings were gone by then. Without our car, we were lost.

Call it a wake-up slap to the side of my face. In that moment of desperation, a fire was lit underneath me. I said to myself, *We are not going to live like this anymore! I am not going to let this happen to our family. Desperation will no longer be a regular part of our vocabulary.* In that instant, my mindset changed from that of a taker to a contributor. From a boy to a man. I didn't know exactly what I would do, but I vowed I would do everything in my power to help.

I grabbed my dad's hand, and the words rushed out of me: "Don't worry! I'm going to work really hard. I'm going to learn how to speak

English. I'm going to make a lot of money. I'm going to buy us a new car, buy us a house, and we're not going to have to worry about rent anymore."

Dad had a younger brother who worked at a restaurant in the Valley. (We hadn't stayed with him because he lived in a camper.) I asked about getting me a job, and he put in a good word for me. I was hired as a busboy. My job was to collect dirty dishes from tables, put them in a rubber tub, and carry them to the dishwasher. *I finally get to contribute*, I told myself. I was really proud. When the dinner crowd thinned out, I leveled the butters and filled up saltshakers.

One evening I was out on the floor collecting dirty dishes, and a woman asked me a question, but I couldn't understand her. My English wasn't great yet. She snapped at me, stood up, and clapped her hands right in my face as if I'd been sleeping. Startled, I took a step back, but she strode forward and got right in my face again, shouting this time. Smacking her hands together again. Calling me an idiot.

That word I knew.

My heart pounded, and I could feel adrenaline coursing through my body. I didn't know what to do. I didn't know what this lady wanted. I ran to the back and got my uncle. He spoke better English than me and came over to her table and asked her what the matter was. She kept pointing at me, glaring like I was some lowlife. My face was red. I felt so small.

She wanted her glass of water refilled. That was it. All she wanted was another glass of water.

That night as I lay in the bedroom I shared with my two sisters, inside the tiny house we could barely afford to rent, after Dad's car had been stolen and he didn't know what to do for work so he could feed and house our family, I renewed my vow. I was going to learn to speak English fluently. I was going to get a better job. No one was going to speak to me like that again. I was going to buy my family a new car, and someday I'd buy us a bigger house, and none of us would need to worry about money ever again. My childhood was over. My adulthood had begun. I'd be dedicated to English, English, English. It was time to put into action all of those lessons I'd tucked away at that early age. Somehow, someway, I was going to lift my family out of this mess.

CHAPTER 3

The Kid with an Accent

Looking back on that low season now, many years later, I see that our car getting stolen spurred me, quite simply, to give myself marching orders, and the whole experience lit a fire under me. Darkness can lead to light if you let it. I stopped killing time with friends on weekends. Soccer took a back seat to my studies, even though I loved the sport. I didn't waste any time with booze (in fact, I didn't have my first drink until I turned twenty-one). I never smoked weed or took drugs. My teenage years were dedicated to working to become everything I vowed I would be.

The police never found Dad's car. He was able to convince a bank to loan him money, so at least he could get something to drive again. Immediately, Dad ramped up his efforts with his side job. Again, he placed another "For Sale" sign in the window and sold his car at a slight profit, then bought a somewhat better car and immediately placed another "For Sale" sign in it, always trying to improve our family's financial position, always trying to stay one step ahead.

I concentrated on my grades, kept busy at my busboy job, and focused on mastering English. One of the hardest and last things to learn are the idioms—*It's raining cats and dogs. Go on a wild-goose chase. Sign your John Hancock.* I didn't know if I'd ever sort them all out.

Money remained tight. Mom shopped only at grocery outlet stores, always with coupons, constantly keeping an eye out for the best deals. Instead of going home with Coca-Cola, we came home with "cola." But hey, it tasted the same. As kids, we were always outgrowing our clothes, and new ones were bought in thrift stores or on sale only. Dad budgeted for gas money, and sometimes toward the end of a month, we couldn't drive anywhere because all the gas money was gone. We never went out to eat anymore. A treat for us was a ninety-nine-cent pizza.

Mom and Dad slowly started settling into their new American life, although their way forward was seldom easy. Dad looked for other jobs, but nothing materialized. Mom reached out to the neighbors and made a friend or two, but I knew she was lonely a lot. Our parents wanted us to make good grades, fit in at school, be able to live our dreams, and stay safe—a constant concern.

As fall 1995 started, Marilyn and I were supposed to attend Birmingham High School in the San Fernando Valley section of Los Angeles, near where we lived. But Birmingham was experiencing a lot of racial tension and fights in those years, so my parents didn't want us there. (A few years later, Birmingham became a charter school, and it's thriving today.) Instead, my parents enrolled us at Taft High School in Woodland Hills, the next town over, a school that placed a strong emphasis on academic and social excellence. The teachers all came highly acclaimed and were known to encourage their students to achieve.

Going to Taft meant that Dad needed to drive us each morning and evening, and we were all mindful of the added expense, even though Dad said it would all somehow work out. The school had an incredibly capable theater program, which intrigued me greatly. I'd heard that Maureen McCormick, who played Marcia on *The Brady Bunch*, had graduated from Taft, as did Susan Olsen, who played her younger sister, Cindy. An artist named O'Shea Jackson Sr. attended Taft a few years ahead of me; known professionally by the stage name Ice Cube, he also went on to have a strong career in music and the movies. Jan Smithers, who played Bailey on *WKRP in Cincinnati*, was a product of Taft, as was Justine Bateman, who starred in *Family Ties*; Lisa Kudrow, who starred in *Friends*; and Robin Wright, who starred in the megahit movies *Forrest Gump* and *The Princess Bride*. Right from the start, I was mindful that Dad was again making a huge effort to give us every advantage this new country offered.

At Taft, I concentrated on my studies, took acting and dancing classes, and appeared in school theater productions. Theater also improved my English. Long gone were the days when a teacher yelled out my parts from backstage.

My participation in theater brought about another benefit: the more I knew English, the more social I became. The more I studied people, the more I saw that pretty much every student was struggling to fit in. It dawned on me that everybody felt insecure in school. Even the coolest kids, who acted like they had it all together. So my approach was that I didn't care what anybody's color was, what language they spoke, or what sport or activity they were into. Everybody's presence was important, and I tried to show that in my interactions. I knew what it felt like to be ignored.

Each morning when Marilyn and I arrived at school, I walked around and said hello to the metalheads at the front entrance, to the sports dudes playing basketball, to the kids just chilling in the cafeteria, and to the surfers and skaters in the quad. At lunchtime, I'd make another round and say hello to everybody again. I had been so shy in middle school—I was making up for lost time. In high school, I became a social butterfly.

Some people still referred to me as "that kid from Venezuela," even though plenty of friends knew my name by now. It's hard to shake off an identity once it's been established, and even though our English was better, I still spoke with a strong accent, while Marilyn's was less pronounced. In middle school, she'd developed several close friendships with kids who spoke perfect English. But back then I'd been friends mostly with my Latino soccer buddies, who didn't help my accent much.

As my sister and I grew in confidence, we felt freer to be ourselves and let our personalities shine. We had been keeping our emotions so tight during those middle-school years that certain parts of us never got the chance to emerge. But overall, those first hard years had made me more empathetic. I realized that when I saw an immigrant kid all by himself in the corner of the lunchroom, keeping his head down, trying so desperately not to draw attention to himself, he could be a really fun friend if given the chance. So I'd walk right up to him and say hello.

Marilyn and I had discovered pretty early on, regretfully, that students in the United States weren't taught a whole lot about world geography and other cultures. It was a sad but true fact, one that's probably still true today. In America, you learn about America. But unless you study or travel overseas for yourself or develop friendships with immigrants, it's hard to experience what other countries and cultures are truly like. Back in middle school, once kids heard we were from Venezuela, they often gave us these perplexed looks like we were fresh out of the jungle. The more confident my sister and I grew, the more we learned to have fun with this, particularly by the time we got to high school.

One day a kid sidled up to us, almost like we were on display at a museum, and asked in an earnest tone, "So, like, are there *schools* in Venezuela?"

Marilyn and I both nodded seriously.

The kid followed up. "Well, like, how did you guys get to school?"

That was my cue. I looked steadily at the kid and answered, completely straight-faced, "We rode donkeys."

Marilyn played along, nodding with a poker face, and I upped my accent slightly and added: "Yes. We rode donkeys everywhere. We did not have grocery stores in Venezuela. So we rode our donkeys to hunt for food. Sometimes we walked during our hunts. Always barefoot. If our feet grew sore, we tied leaves around our feet. Our favorite food was elephant."

The kid's jaw dropped to the floor.

We figured out we could spin these stories until our answers became outrageous, and finally the kid would break in and say, "Wait a minute. You're not serious, right?" It always set us off laughing. And it helped break the ice. The kids would laugh then, too, and they'd realize we were all pretty much the same.

A FEW MONTHS INTO MY FRESHMAN YEAR AT TAFT, MY acting teacher pulled me aside one afternoon and said, "Hey, Wilmer, you're pretty good. You take acting seriously. If you auditioned for commercials, I bet you could land some spots."

I was like, "Wait a minute," and my eyes lit up like dollar signs. Commercials would be far more fun than working as a busboy. Besides, the money I dreamed about wouldn't be for me. If I could earn some extra cash, I would help my family.

"How do you break into commercials?" I asked.

"Well, you need to go to auditions, and a lot of them," my teacher said. "You could start going on your own right now. But it would help to have a few extra classes under your belt to get specific training for commercials. With extra classes, you'd also meet more people in the industry."

I nodded, trying to take it all in. Taft didn't offer extra classes, and I wasn't sure where to get them, but I didn't have the gumption to ask. A few evenings later I was listening to the radio at home. During a lull in the music, I heard an announcer say with a deep voice, "Are you between the ages of thirteen and eighteen and interested in appearing in television and the movies? Come to the Hilton Hotel by Los Angeles International Airport this weekend for an acting showcase. We're picking the next stars of tomorrow."

I grabbed a pencil and scribbled down the details. I hated to ask Dad if he could drive me over and sign me up. I knew it would cost something. But I screwed up my courage, went into the living room, and presented the classes to him as a potential investment. He thought for a minute, then, to my joy, he agreed, provided I kept my grades up. I had straight As in school by then. By Dad's tone, I sensed he considered the extra acting classes would become more like another hobby of mine, like soccer. But I planned to take them as seriously as a heart attack.

The extra classes began. The rest of the students and I did table reads and received specific training for commercials, but the training was limited, and I wanted more. An instructor named Celeste Boyd spotted my potential. A middle-aged Black woman as beautiful as Lauryn Hill, she offered additional lessons on Wednesday nights at her house and invited me to join her advanced class. All ages attended, and it would be good for me to work with adults, she said, not just with kids my age.

I said thanks but no thanks. I couldn't go. The truth was that Dad's wallet was tapped out, and I knew asking him for more money was out of the question. Ms. Boyd had already sensed my drive—and she must have picked up on my financial need—because she sort of looked me up and down and said, "No problem. I want to teach you for free. I really think you can do this."

I thought quickly. "Can I bring my sister too?" I wanted Marilyn to have whatever goodness came my way.

Ms. Boyd paused, laughed, then said, "Sure, why not?"

Celeste Boyd became one of the best teachers I'd ever encountered. She had a passion for using the power of the arts to inspire her students, and I absolutely loved her class. Thanks to her teaching, I discovered I could do serious acting. I could be funny. I could perform other voices just like I did when I was a child—but this time much more convincingly. She empowered me to discover my true talents. I could make the class cry or laugh or feel afraid or happy, sometimes with only a facial gesture.

One day I was performing a scene when I noticed her staring at me, thoughtfully. When I finished, she said, "Wilmer, that is very good. You're ready to go out there and work as an actor and do very well." She offered to introduce me to an agent friend of hers. He led a smaller-sized agency, but it was legitimate, and he regularly came to her classes to find new actors. He was going to show up the following week. I grinned. She gave me a scene to study.

The next week, her agent friend attended, and I poured my heart into performing the scene. Afterward, he talked with me and said I had potential. But no, he wouldn't represent me formally. Instead, he would send me on a couple of auditions to see what kind of feedback we got. If the feedback was good, we'd talk about representation then.

I auditioned for everything he sent me on—four auditions for commercials and two for one-line parts in TV shows. One casting director called me "incredible." Another said, "He's so free and fun." Another said, "He came in extremely committed and prepared." Still another said, "He's phenomenal." But no offers came. Despite my talent, every single casting agent highlighted one big problem.

This kid has an accent.

The agent sat me down and gave it to me straight. Placing me any-where was going to be an uphill battle. When it came to commercials, TV shows, and movies in the 1990s, parts for teenage Latino actors, particularly those with strong accents, were few and far between. Mario Lopez had played A.C. Slater in the hit TV show *Saved by the Bell*, but the series ended in 1993, and he'd spoken English flawlessly. Wilson Cruz played Rickie Vasquez in *My So-Called Life*, but that had ended in 1995, and his English was perfect. Mayteana Morales had played a character called Gaby Fernández in a PBS series called *Ghostwriter* in the early 1990s. Again, perfect English. He couldn't think of anyone else around my age who'd broken in.

When it came to parts for adult-aged Latino actors, he explained they were just as rare. Who else with an accent was a household name in the United States besides Desi Arnaz? The legendary Ricardo Montalbán had been a big star with *Fantasy Island*, but that show had ended in 1984. Jimmy Smits had a breakout role playing Victor Sifuentes in *L.A. Law* until 1992, but he spoke perfect English. A former telenovela actress named Salma Hayek had starred in a few American movies, but it would be years still before she became a household name. Benicio del Toro had acted in a few movies, but he wasn't a big name yet. Antonio Banderas had just broken through with his roles in *Philadelphia*, *Assassins*, and *Desperado*. But he was one in a million.

How was I ever going to break in? The agent shrugged. I went on more auditions. But soon I discovered that if a Latino did land a role, it was always for one or two lines only, and almost always to play a bad guy. The Latino actors played the criminals, the gangsters, the killers, the drug dealers. Plus, you had to look like a bad guy to get the part. A shaved head helped. So did tattoos. And a really muscular physique. A clean-cut skinny kid like me was at the end of the line.

Roles for teens were even harder to land than for adults—and there were plenty of adults for any casting director to choose from. The numbers didn't lie. On every audition I went on, I took notes, listening to the industry insiders talk. I learned there were something like twenty thousand actors actually working at any one time in the United States, plus another hundred thousand unemployed members of the actors' union who were all hoping to land roles, plus as many as one hundred to two hundred thousand aspiring actors like me who didn't belong to the union and hadn't landed any roles yet.

Looking at the statistics was depressing, and my dream seemed almost impossible. I'd been trying to learn English for three years. I kept going to all these cattle-call auditions, where everyone is invited to try out, week after week after week, and the casting directors kept asking me to speak like every kid in America. I could do incredible impersonations of any number of celebrities. But the one thing I couldn't impersonate was a kid who spoke perfect English.

MY FRESHMAN YEAR OF HIGH SCHOOL PASSED, AND MY sophomore year began. I kept going to more and more auditions, always hoping for one lucky break. I was oblivious to any national conversations about diversity, inclusion, and representation that may have been happening back then. Or maybe the conversations simply weren't happening to any significant degree. But anyway, I wasn't looking for a break because of being a minority; I didn't even see myself so much that way. I didn't walk in the front door with a big sign around my neck that announced my ethnicity. I was simply an actor in an ocean of actors, so I tried to use anything to my advantage. If other actors could break through, then maybe I could too. If I prepared my ass off, if I got up earlier in the morning than everybody else, if I kept knocking on doors, why couldn't I at least have the same shot as everybody else?

By the time I was halfway through my sophomore year, I'd figured out lots about the industry on my own. The best auditions weren't the cattle calls. Let's face it, you might be the next Tom Cruise, but if three thousand teenagers were all trying out for the same part, even if you made it to the top ten, you still wouldn't get hired. You might have been better than 2,990 other actors, but you had to be number one to land the part. So I learned that the best auditions were the ones where there was a sign out front that read, "Agent Submissions Only." These were closed auditions with fewer actors trying out. Your agent worked to get you in the door.

Well, I wasn't daunted. The first time I went to an audition like this—on my own—my heart was pounding so hard. I grabbed the appropriate paperwork, then stood by myself in a corner, hoping like hell I wouldn't get caught. The first blank space was easy. All I had to do was fill out my John Hancock. I carefully wrote "Wilmer Eduardo Valderrama." The next blank was more difficult. It asked for my agency. I thought hard. The name needed to sound American and easily forgotten. I knew there were eight main agencies in Hollywood at the time (UTA, APA, CAA, ICM, William Morris, Endeavor, Paradigm, and Gersh) and that all these big agencies easily employed a couple thousand agents. Then there were countless smaller to midsize agencies and a couple thousand agents who worked for those companies too. No way would a casting agent know every agency's name in Los Angeles. I thought again, then carefully wrote, "Smith and Associates." That name was sure to fly under the radar.

The next blank was for my nonexistent sending agent's phone number. I scratched my head. The phone didn't ring a lot in our house, so I wrote down our home number. If it rang, I could sprint to the phone or teach my sisters to answer, "Smith and Associates, how can I help you?"

But there was a final hurdle. To prepare for these roles, the other actors would receive their scripts from their agents ahead of time, a luxury I didn't have. I'd made it inside the front door, but what was I going to do now? As I stood in line, I watched and listened to the actors ahead of me rehearse. Carefully but fast, I scrambled to memorize what they were saying. When it came time for me to audition, I knew the lines. But no, I didn't land that first part. I sighed. After all my best cunning, and again knowing I did well on the lines, I was turned down again. Still, I came away with some new strategies.

Over the months to come, I hustled a lot of auditions that way and sometimes even got callbacks. Still, nothing was landing. I kept auditioning, month after month. Always being rejected. Always hearing the word *no*. Then, in late spring of my sophomore year, I auditioned for a tiny part in a Pacific Bell Smart Yellow Pages ad. A regional commercial. My job was to look straight into the camera with all the intensity I could muster and say, "Pacific Bell Smart Yellow Pages." It was only one line, but I was sure I gave it an Oscar-worthy performance.

And I actually landed the commercial!

I had never imagined the feeling of walking out the door with a check in hand—an absolute victory—after I'd tried so hard and failed so many times. For that single commercial, they paid me a couple thousand bucks. I talked to my dad, and he told me to keep the investment going. With the money I made from that commercial, I was able to pay for one year's membership in the Screen Actors Guild. That meant I could audition for larger parts. But the clock was ticking. If I didn't land something within a year, I couldn't pay my dues again.

A couple weeks later, thanks to my SAG membership, I was able to audition for a CBS miniseries called *Four Corners*. Another wonder: I landed a small part playing Antonio, the autistic son of one of the main characters. These days, there are beautiful autistic actors who do their own work, but back then, casting directors auditioned regular actors for such roles. To prepare, I researched autism extensively and learned as many mannerisms as I could. Then I gave it my all. The people on set were convinced by my performance, and several asked if I was actually autistic. The miniseries starred the legendary Swedish American actress Ann-Margret, and even she was convinced. I felt honored just to be in the same room with her. The casting agent loved how I played the character and brought me in to audition for more parts on other shows. Again, I received a lot of great feedback, but again I kept getting rejected. It was always the same problem.

This kid has an accent.

A couple of months passed. I auditioned for a tiny part in a Japanese commercial. It didn't even have any lines, and I landed the role, but it was too little, too late. All this auditioning was costing Dad gas money, and my union membership was almost up. The money I made from the Japanese commercial wasn't enough to pay for another year. I took the bus to my auditions as often as I could, and sometimes I'd take two buses, even three. But Dad often drove me if an audition was far away, and each dollar he made was becoming increasingly precious.

That January, we were late on rent. Dad hustled a few more errands for the auto parts stores, and we were able to make rent within the window it was due. But in February, Dad was late on rent again. Again, we scraped by in the nick of time—I thought. In March, we were late for a third time, and this time the landlord knocked on our door. It was dark outside, and Dad had just gotten home from work and was sitting on the couch, exhausted. He glanced at the door, then looked at me. I started to get up to answer the door, but Dad shook his head. I gave him a puzzled look.

"*Mijo*," he said, "this evening we are not home."

Dad wasn't breaking even. He explained quietly that we still hadn't paid February's rent. We were actually two months behind. Mom came into the room and took Dad's hand. I could see the desperation in my parents' eyes. We had no idea what to do.

CHAPTER 4

Teenage Wasteland

W e were at the bottom. It was our darkest season. Maybe my acting dream had been one of those wild-goose chase things.

In the spring of my junior year—I was eighteen, running on empty—an agent sent me on an audition for a TV pilot called *Teenage Wasteland*. I didn't put much stock into the show at first. I vowed to give it my all, just like everything else. But after you've been auditioning for a few years without much success, you learn not to get your hopes up. I knew that around five hundred pilots are pitched each season. Most pitches, even if they're heard by network and studio execs, never see the light of day. From those five hundred, maybe seventy pilot scripts are ordered each year, and from those, maybe eight or nine will be picked up as new shows. Even then, few shows will finish out the first season without getting canceled early. I'd long since learned that television is an industry where failure is the norm. It's a business of gambling. You have to audition a lot. Pitch a lot. Try a lot. Throw those dice a lot. Executives and actors have to make a ton of pilots that go straight into the trash with the hope that one in five hundred—maybe more like one in five thousand—will ever become a hit.

The initial audition for *Teenage Wasteland* was in Studio City, and I took the bus. At the studio, the floor was full of kids. I gathered that the early buzz for the show was strong, and it seemed that every teenage actor in Los Angeles was auditioning for this one. I recognized a few faces—a kid I knew from the *Mighty Morphin Power Rangers.* Another friend who'd done some morning shows. But almost everybody was unknown. For this pilot, the casting agents wanted fresh faces.

I was an old hand at auditioning by then, so I knew the dynamic of the situation. When you're waiting to audition, you seldom talk to other actors. Sure, there's a sense that you're all in this together— you're all struggling at the same time, and you hope to see other people succeed. But there's also a big sense of competing with each other. You're like sprinters at a starting line, everybody feeling the nerves, all waiting for the starter pistol to crack. Truly, everybody is scared out of their mind.

While I was waiting, tapping my foot and going over my lines for the umpteenth time, a tall, skinny kid with a shock of dark hair walked into the room, opened a fridge, grabbed a bottle of water, and began to drink it.

Something about his actions rubbed me the wrong way. *That's not his water,* I thought. *That's not his fridge. That is so disrespectful. This guy is* definitely *not getting the part.* Little did I know that this actor had already auditioned multiple times and landed one of the lead roles. He was just coming in to do chemistry reads—where the casting director sees how he connects with other actors. Some other kid knew him and called him by a first name I hadn't heard before in America. The name sounded weird, starting with a *T* but rhyming with *gopher.* That wasn't quite it. *Tofu,* maybe?

I threw my heart into the audition, although Tofu didn't read with me. It was someone else. They don't give you the full script for the pilot when you audition. They give you a couple of scenes, and you have to miraculously come up with a character and decide how he should be played. The only thing I'd been told was that I'd be playing a foreign exchange student who just arrived in the United States, struggled to understand English, and didn't understand the culture. (I could relate in a big way.) They didn't specify an ethnicity, and they indicated that the character might not be given an actual name. I went in and used my own accent in the first audition, trying to play with the lines the best I knew how. I seemed to be getting some laughs, although the laughs didn't seem that loud. I figured they were only being polite.

"We'll call you if we're interested in another audition," someone said. "If you come in again, just relax and have fun with this character. Okay?"

I nodded. Feedback like that meant I'd probably played the character too on the nose. Too obvious. That meant I'd blown it, particularly with this many actors auditioning. Nothing had stood out about my performance.

I didn't want to turn my back on them when I was walking out the door, because I thought that might be disrespectful. In complete sincerity, I backed out of the room while keeping my front toward them. A few of them laughed again, perhaps thinking I was still trying to play the character. But how could I know? Maybe they thought I was a weirdo.

A COUPLE OF DAYS PASSED, AND THE PRODUCERS called me back for a second audition. This was a good sign, but plenty of auditions have callbacks, so it could mean anything. I certainly didn't get my hopes up.

At home, I started running through my lines again, experimenting with different accents from other parts of the world, combining bits and pieces of them together. I knew I needed something larger, broader, smarter, something that would deepen this character's dynamic and totally knock my second audition out of the park.

I started with my own Venezuelan accent and added a touch of my mother's from Colombia. I thought a bit, then layered on the rolling of the *r*'s from South America. I thought some more, then added a lisp, traditionally thought to be from Spain. It isn't so much a lisp as it is a quickening of the voice in certain locations. It's hard to describe unless you've heard it. Both the *z* and *c* consonants are pronounced with an unvoiced *th*. Like, if I said, "kitchen sink," I'd say it as a very quick "kitchen *th*ink." The character was strengthening, but something still wasn't quite right. "Just relax and have fun," they'd told me. I scratched my head. How could I relax and have fun when so much was on the line? I was trying to make this the absolute funniest character anybody had ever seen!

I took a break to think some more and walked into the kitchen to get a glass of water. My youngest sister, Stephanie, was doing her homework at the kitchen table, and I tried out some of my lines on her. She was ten by then, and I was always super relaxed around her, the same way I was around Marilyn. But Stephanie could be a tough audience, too, in the sense she wouldn't laugh at just anything I said anymore, like she'd done when she was a little kid. She could be a good test audience.

When I tried the material in my regular voice, Stephanie kept a straight face. She'd heard my normal voice a million times, and nothing was funny about it to her. I kept talking, gradually blending in the mix of accents I'd prepared. Still, she didn't laugh. I rolled a few r's. I lisped a few z's. Nothing. This new accent wasn't doing it for her.

I began to say any old knucklehead thing, trying out any number of sounds and pitches that came to me on the fly. Suddenly, I started speaking in a new lilting, higher-pitched voice that didn't match my personality. I spoke with a bit of an underbite, sometimes raising an eyebrow, and letting my mouth go relaxed, occasionally doing a slight duckface with my lips. I didn't know exactly where any of it came from. This new voice was singsong. Goofy. Wacky.

Stephanie started cracking up.

I mean, she started laughing like this was the most hilarious thing she'd ever heard. I kept at it, saying anything and everything I could in this new voice. It didn't matter what I said, she kept giggling her head off. The voice sounded disarming and naive. The character could be from anywhere. And I noticed that I could deliberately fumble lines and stay in character. Stephanie laughed and laughed. I thought, *Okay, maybe I'm on to something here.*

That night I stayed awake for a long time, thinking through this new voice and the upcoming audition. The voice was so exaggerated that it might be exactly the secret sauce this character needed. Yet then again, it might be pushed too far. I didn't want to be totally off base when I went in for the audition. The voice was almost cartoonish. Perhaps I'd be pushing the envelope too much. It would be a gamble.

When I walked into the second audition, I smiled and looked around the room. About fifteen producers and cocreators were seated around tables. I didn't know anybody by name. I was scared out of my mind, and running through my head still was the big question: *Should I use this new voice?*

I took a deep breath and launched. The moment I said my first line, the room exploded. They were laughing as hard as Stephanie had.

I was still scared, because I didn't know if the laughing was good or bad. Maybe they were laughing at me.

I ran through all my lines using this new voice, and when I finished, someone said, "Thanks for coming in." That's all the feedback they gave me. Some of them were still laughing. I'd either completely nailed this audition or I'd completely bombed it. Again, I didn't want to turn my back on them. So just like the last time, I backed out of the room while keeping my front toward them. They all kept laughing.

THE COMPETITION WAS SO FIERCE THAT I WAS CALLED back for a third audition. I wasn't fazed by three auditions, because a lot of shows have more than one, although three is a lot. Again, I decided to use the newer voice, and again I heard a ton of laughter. Again, I was unsure if that was good or not.

Finally, they called me in for a fourth audition. This one was in Century City at a different studio, a bit farther away, and would mean a longer bus ride. Dad was broke, but I think he sensed something bigger was brewing. He literally borrowed gas money from our neighbors and drove me over.

By that time I knew the industry protocol, that before you audition for a TV pilot, they make you sign a contract, which tells an actor exactly how much you'll make if hired. This contract said I'd make $15,000 for the pilot. If the pilot was picked up, I'd make $10,000 for each following episode.

On the drive over for my fourth audition, I thought about the contract, looked at my father, and with an incredulous chuckle said, "Dad, can you imagine if I got this part right now—we'd be rich!" Fifteen thousand dollars was more than we made in a whole year.

Without missing a beat, he said in his low gravel voice, "*Mijo*, if you get it, very good. And if you don't get it, very good." The message was clear: he loved and supported me either way.

In the hallway for the fourth audition, I spotted a tall girl with strawberry blonde hair. She was auditioning for the role of a character named Donna. I also spotted a middle-aged actress with shoulder-length hair who was auditioning to be the mother of the family on the show. I thought I recognized her from somewhere—maybe she'd had a bit part in *Big* with a young Tom Hanks, but I wasn't sure.

I figured I had nothing to lose, so I just went for it. I started talking in the newer voice that had made Stephanie laugh, and they were all laughing so hard in the audition room I couldn't hear the casting director read the lines with me. I literally had to read her lips and wait for her to stop so I could say my lines.

In the first scene, a bunch of teenage friends were hanging out at a restaurant. One of the girls needed to go to the bathroom and insisted that a girlfriend go with her. That was my cue. I stood, looked at the lead character, and said, "I, too, must go to the bathroom . . . Eric?" Everybody in the room laughed. The person reading for Eric shook his head and answered, "It doesn't work that way with guys." Again, everybody laughed.

In the next scene, I was sitting in a basement in a circle with three other guys, munching on snacks. We just happened to be hanging out in a mysteriously smoky room, although it was never explained where the smoke came from. (It could have been a smoking refrigerator. I mean, who really knew?) The guys were complaining about the high price of gasoline while discussing the possibility of the main character getting to use his parents' station wagon. Two of the guys referred to the station wagon as a boat, to which I asked, very innocently, "Who's getting a *boat*?" Everyone in the room laughed.

One of the guys wondered aloud if he could borrow gas money from his girlfriend, to which Eric shook his head in disgust and said to him, "You're such a whore." The camera panned to me, and I asked Eric, thinking this is a word that American guys used for other guys, "When does the boat get here, *whore*?" Everybody in the room howled.

In the final audition scene, the gang was stuck at a gas station where their car had broken down. The lead character remarked that he had to listen to one of the girls complain for an hour, to which I piped up and said, in deliberately almost unintelligible English, "A really long hour." Everybody laughed.

Another character, the one with the girlfriend, was also feeling the strain of waiting and deadpanned the line, "God hates me." And I quipped back to the guy, very innocently, "How can you say God hates you? At least you have a woman's love. Be happy . . . *whore*." Everybody cracked up.

At this fourth audition, I absolutely swung for the fences. I mean, I auditioned my ass off. When I was finished, one of the show's creators stood and started clapping. I didn't know what she meant. Maybe it was a one-woman standing ovation. Or maybe she thought I was off my rocker, and she wanted to do something polite so I'd get out of there fast. "Thank you so very much for coming in today," was all she said.

I was still scared out of my mind. I left the audition room and the waiting started, because they never tell you anything at first. Dad and I climbed back into his car and went to pick up a ninety-nine-cent pizza for our family for dinner.

I wasn't sure if a call would ever come. If it did, there was only a slim chance it could be good news, but most likely it would be bad, just like the results of all my other auditions.

That same night, shortly after my family had finished our cardboardy pizza, the phone rang. I shot a glance to Dad. He looked at Mom. She looked at my sisters. I ran to pick it up. Very slowly, the agent said, "Hey, Wilmer, they want you to come back tomorrow . . ."

I gasped. Then shuddered. Maybe they just wanted me to come in again for another callback.

Before I could ask, the agent continued, ". . . and they want you to keep coming back the day after that . . . and the day after that . . . and the day after that."

I let go of the receiver and shouted the news. "I got the part!" Mom and Dad hugged each other. Marilyn started cheering. Stephanie started crying. We all hugged each other. All of our emotions mixed together. Crying. Cheering. Shouting. It was absolute pandemonium. This was the American dream unfolding for us, the crucial next step in our upward climb. I took a breath and looked out the window into the evening Los Angeles sky. An American flag flew in front of our neighbor's house, and I lingered for a split second in the enormous symbolism of this moment. I knew it now. I knew it without a doubt. Everything was possible in this new country of ours. The American dream was achievable for anyone who comes to this country with a hope that isn't possible in the country they left. My doorway had opened. All I had to do was not get fired from the pilot. Even if the pilot didn't get picked up, I had just made $15,000. That was rent for our family for the rest of the year. We were "rich!"

I went to the tiny bedroom I still shared with my sisters, looked in the mirror, and made another vow to myself: *I won't let down my family. I have been given a chance to lift us all, and I won't blow this incredible opportunity. Every performance I give will be the absolute best that anyone has ever seen. Soon, we will get a new car. A new house. We will eat at restaurants again.* I just knew it.

I went to the pilot and put my whole heart into each scene. The pilot finished taping. That same evening, I took my mother to a regular grocery store, not the discount store. She was able to buy all the brand names she wanted. Not the knockoffs. That was a start. Then we all waited on pins and needles to see if the pilot would get picked up.

A call didn't come the first night. Or the second. Or the third. A week passed. Then another. This wasn't good. *Probably another one got away.*

Finally, a call came. But when the agent started talking, he didn't sound optimistic. He said, "Well, I'm afraid we have some good news and some bad news."

My heart sunk. "What's the bad news? Give that to me first."

"I'm sorry to tell you that *Teenage Wasteland* is no more." He gave a long pause. "They changed the name of the series to *That '70s Show.*"

I waited. The bad news didn't seem very bad at all.

He continued, his voice rising in excitement, "The good news is the show got picked up for thirteen episodes. Congratulations, Wilmer, you're going straight to network television!"

CHAPTER 5

That '70s Show

Other than my mother being able to shop at Ralphs, life didn't change much for our family immediately after work began on *That '70s Show*. I still had another year to go in high school, and I'd promised my dad I would finish high school no matter what. He hadn't been able to finish high school himself, and I had this dream of me walking across the stage at graduation, being handed my diploma, then walking off the stage and giving my diploma to my dad as a tribute. I wasn't sure how I would juggle full-time high school with a full-time job, but I promised myself I wasn't going to let him down.

Right before the pilot had been made, the producers had invited everyone to a cast dinner at an upscale restaurant in Studio City. It was spring 1998, and this was before we'd had any rehearsals or wardrobe fittings or met anyone on a soundstage. I had my driver's license by then, but Dad decided he was going to take me that evening. We pulled up to the curb in the old Ford Taurus station wagon that Dad had traded up to by that time, and he let me out. The color of the hood didn't match the color of the car's body, but it was our family's limousine. I stared at my dad for one long moment. I sensed a new season of life lay before me, one that could greatly benefit our whole family, but he wasn't saying anything. He just nodded his head, man to man, like he was proud of me. That was more than enough. I closed the car door and walked inside.

The room was packed with strangers. Right away, I recognized the kid who had opened the fridge back at auditions and had grabbed the bottled water. *Man, I can't believe he got the part*, I thought. Turned out his name was Topher Grace. He'd been cast in the lead role of Eric Forman, and he greeted me with a warm smile. Maybe he was going to be okay after all.

I recognized the tall girl with the strawberry blonde hair from auditions—Laura Prepon. She'd been cast as Donna Pinciotti, the next-door neighbor and love interest of Eric Forman. I learned in talking to her later that Laura was originally from New Jersey. Her dad had been an orthopedic surgeon, but he'd died five years earlier during his own heart surgery. Laura had been thirteen years old when he passed, and I knew even then that the death of a parent is incredibly hard on a kid. That difficult fact of Laura's life endeared her to me immediately. I couldn't relate to losing my father, but I certainly knew what it was like for my parents to go through hard times.

The middle-aged woman from the auditions milled around near the front of the restaurant. Debra Jo Rupp had been cast as the show's mother, Kitty Forman. Debra had been born in California, she told me, but had lived in New York most recently, where she'd starred in a bunch of on- and off-Broadway plays. I could see right away that she had a genuinely upbeat personality and a friendly laugh. I liked her from the start, and the more I got to know her, the more she seemed just like a real-life mom.

I looked toward the bar and did a double take. Sitting casually on a barstool was none other than Kurtwood Smith—the bad guy from *RoboCop*. I thought he might be visiting someone at the restaurant, because he was talking to one of the show's writers like he knew him. It didn't cross my mind that he might be part of the cast. I absolutely needed to meet him. Walking up to Kurtwood, my palms went sweaty, and I wondered what to say. The writer seemed to know me already, because he introduced me to Kurtwood, and I managed to stammer, "S-sir . . . I know all the lines to *RoboCop*," and I launched into my best rendition of "H-hey, now wait a second. Now, wait a minute. You're taking this kind of personal, aren't ya? Come on, man. Come on, now. You're making me nervous. Come on, you can't do this! Come on, now! Don't mess around!"[1]

Kurtwood laughed heartily, shook my hand, and said with a head nod, "I'm looking forward to it." But that was one of those English idioms I didn't understand yet. I was about to ask what he meant, but a producer called us all over to the table to eat. Surprise! Kurtwood rose from his barstool and started walking with me toward the table, like we were old friends. My mind did somersaults and I wondered, *Why is Kurtwood Smith walking next to me?!* At the table, he pulled out the chair next to him and motioned for me to sit, and I was like, *Why is Kurtwood Smith wanting me to sit next to him?* I was so nervous I couldn't ask questions.

A producer stood to make a toast, but first he asked us all to go around the table and say our real names and what character we each were playing. One by one, each person stood. "Hi, I'm Mila Kunis, and I'm playing Jackie Burkhart." "Hi, I'm Ashton Kutcher, and I'm playing Michael Kelso." "Hi, I'm Wilmer Valderrama, and I'm playing FES." Kurtwood stood. "Hi, I'm Kurtwood Smith. I'm playing Red Forman, the father on the show."

You're on the show?! I screamed in my mind. *The same show as me? I think this show is going to be legit!*

That night was only the beginning of living my dreams. Being on the same show with an on-screen legend from my boyhood years back in Venezuela was simply a bonus of the whole experience. After the pilot was made and the show was picked up, Kurtwood and I eventually became great friends. I'd call him up and leave messages on his answering machine, just for fun, doing a perfect gritty Clarence Boddicker from *RoboCop*.

"Can you fly, Bobby?"

TO THIS DAY, SO MANY YEARS LATER, I'M NOT EXACTLY sure how *That '70s Show* came to be born. I've heard stories over the years, and a few myths have probably crept into the telling, because that's how it works in Hollywood. But what I've come to understand is that TV shows have family trees, and one of our long-lost ancestors was *Saturday Night Live*.

In the beginning, the husband-and-wife team of Terry and Bonnie Turner were lead writers on *SNL*. They penned sketches for the best comics of that generation, including Dan Aykroyd, Jane Curtin, Chris Farley, David Spade, Mike Myers, Dana Carvey, and Phil Hartman. Then the Turners ventured out from *SNL* to write a string of hit movies, including *Wayne's World*, *Coneheads*, *Tommy Boy*, and *The Brady Bunch Movie*. Along the way, the Turners developed a strong affinity for the 1970s. They loved the groovy style of the era, tie-dyed shirts, flowers, beads, and bell-bottoms. They'd also created a hit TV show called *3rd Rock from the Sun*, just before creating ours, and one of the consulting writers on that show was the ever-brilliant Mark Brazill, a former stand-up comedian who also loved the 1970s.

The Turners and Mark decided to develop a modern coming-of-age show set twenty years behind the times—a 1990s show set in the 1970s—much the same way *Happy Days* had been written in the 1970s but set in the 1950s. The more that Mark shared his personal story with the Turners, the more they became inspired by Mark's real life. He'd grown up as a loner, a sincere and warmhearted everyman struggling to find himself. The real-life Mark Brazill morphed into the character of Eric Forman.

Bonnie had grown up outside Toledo in the type of one-horse town where a group of high school friends has nothing better to do except hang out with each other. Her hometown became the inspiration for the fictional Point Place, Wisconsin, the setting of *That '70s Show*. That kind of town didn't call for plots full of adventure like, say, the setting of *Miami Vice*. It offered introspection. Point Place invited its characters to sit around in a basement and talk. It provided an endless opportunity for the characters to create their own fun.

Terry and Mark both had been reared by tough, grouchy, no-nonsense fathers, so they intrinsically knew what it was like to be the son of such a dad. That became the inspiration for Red Forman, Eric's dad. The other main characters—a beautiful girl next door, a stuck-up cheerleader, a stoner, a naive jock so good-looking it caused him problems—these were archetypes found in every high school in America, and they became the basis of Donna, Jackie, Hyde, and Kelso. Back in high school, Bonnie had been friends with a foreign exchange student. He became the inspiration for Fez, my character. (Actually, we spelled his name "FES" at the start—an acronym for "Foreign Exchange Student.")

The Turners and Mark joined forces with Marcy Carsey and Tom Werner, who'd started a production company called Carsey-Werner. That was the other side of our show's family tree. Marcy and Tom had cut their teeth as programming executives at ABC, shepherding such hits as *Happy Days, Barney Miller, Mork and Mindy, Taxi, Dynasty,* and *Soap.* The way I heard it, Marcy had been full of determination to start a company she owned, and I took quiet notes when I first heard about it, wondering if I could do a similar thing someday myself. She left ABC in 1980, took out a loan, and started her own production company. That took courage, for sure. Less than a year later, Tom joined the company, and they soon had a string of hits, including *Oh Madeline* (starring Madeline Kahn); *The Cosby Show*; and its spin-off, *A Different World*. Then *Roseanne*, *Grace Under Fire*, and *Cybill*. They were also producing *3rd Rock from the Sun*. More people were involved in our show's creation, but that's the bare bones.

When I'd first gone to audition, I'd heard that our show's creators had aimed to cast unknowns, but what I didn't realize until later was how far and wide they'd actually searched. They'd held auditions everywhere—New York; Miami; Chicago; Washington, DC; Dallas; Hollywood. You name it. They'd looked at thousands of kids. And they'd ended up with a cast full of potential, they told us soon after the show had been picked up. *That '70s Show* had everything going for it from the start, and as actors, every one of us had the potential to break out and become a star. Most importantly, we could be a part of something worthwhile.

Sometimes people hear the word *sitcom* and think it's on the low end of the entertainment food chain. But I've learned that a sitcom can be far more intellectual and influential than people initially think. We had the opportunity not only to reflect a culture of a bygone era, they told us, but to comment on and shape the current culture we were part of. If a sitcom breaks out and becomes a hit, it can influence fashion, style, and culture. Catchphrases infiltrate the language and become the insider jokes of a generation. Families, neighbors, and colleagues can be drawn together by sitcoms. People in lunchrooms across America talk about sitcoms the morning after they air.

Sitcoms can even shape values. They can dismantle and rebuild worldviews. They can introduce characters who represent minority and marginalized people groups, perhaps some that America hasn't seen up close before, and bring these people groups into the mainstream.

Perhaps most importantly, sitcoms exist to make people laugh. At their core, they make life better by bringing joy to audiences.

We had the opportunity to do all that, to do something really important—and it was gonna be fun.

THE FIRST EPISODE OF *THAT '70S SHOW* WAS SET TO debut on August 23, 1998, and we all went to work like mad to prepare for the filming. There's a lot to learn at first, and everybody jumped in to figure out the intricacies of their character and how as an ensemble we could all relate to each other.

We were supposed to be high school students with a couple of years left before graduation. In real life, Topher was a student at USC and would turn twenty that July. I was eighteen and finishing eleventh grade. Ashton was twenty and had been a student at the University of Iowa in biochemical engineering. Laura had just turned eighteen and had already worked as a model, doing photo shoots in Paris, Milan, and South America. Danny Masterson, who played the stoner Hyde, was the oldest at twenty-two and the only one of us kids with any sitcom experience, previously playing a character called Justin on *Cybill*.

The truth about Mila's age didn't come out until later. Back during auditions, when asked how old she was, she'd said with a smile, "I'm going to turn eighteen." She'd delivered all her lines flawlessly and landed the role. The show's creators loved her for the part. She was perfect. But when it came time for her to sign her contract, she asked in the fine print to have a "studio teacher." One of the producers asked, "What exactly do you mean?"

"Oh, you know," Mila said with a shrug. "I'll need a teacher on set because, well . . . I'm actually . . . um . . . fourteen."

The way I heard it, a lot of jaws dropped.

Mila insisted she hadn't lied. Not technically. One day, in a few years, she explained, she was indeed going to turn eighteen.

Bonnie and Terry Turner respected her so much as an actor they kept her on.

ON A FREE DAY IN SPRING 1998, NEAR THE END OF ELEVenth grade, I met with all my teachers and explained that I'd be working full-time on a new sitcom, and they all indicated that if I got my work turned in and took the tests and passed them, I could miss class when I needed to be at the studio—which was a lot. I wasn't positive if I was headed for a career in acting. I valued education and wanted to graduate from high school. I liked psychology a lot, and that was a field I was considering. I was also enamored with the thought of being a pilot for the US Air Force, and I knew I'd need a college degree for that. For now I was acting, and I was throwing my heart into it.

Truly, my schedule was nutty that spring—and also for my entire senior year. The show would shoot every day for two weeks. Then we'd have a week off. Then three weeks on, one week off, two weeks on, one week off, three on again. I went to school on my weeks off. During my weeks on, Marilyn communicated with my teachers and figured out what I needed to do, then I'd rush around to do all my schoolwork, and Marilyn carried my assignments back to school for me.

Transportation was always a chore, particularly because Taft High School wasn't the school that Marilyn and I were supposed to go to, so no school buses ran from our house to Taft. That left public transportation or Dad. I didn't have my own car yet, and although I loved cars, I was hesitant to get my own set of wheels so soon. I definitely wouldn't get one before the show was picked up, and even after that I would be cautious. It could get canceled at any time. Where would that leave my family financially?

Dad was good about driving us whenever he could. A few times I even drove his car to school or the studio by myself. But often I'd take the bus, and I had to transfer halfway and take two different buses to school. Dad had a particularly busy season that spring, so I was riding the bus a lot. The network was also doing a ton of advertising for the show. One morning I stepped up to take the bus to school and—no joke—that stinking bus was wrapped all the way around with a huge advertisement for *That '70s Show*. I climbed off the bus near my high school, and my face was on the same bus that I was riding in! Kids were like, "What?!"

That spring of 1998, the sitcom *Seinfeld* was finishing its ninth and final season. The show was absolutely huge, and Jerry Seinfeld was reportedly the first television actor to earn a million bucks per episode. I'd heard some friends talking at school about *Seinfeld* being shot in New York, which they assumed because the show is set in that city. But actually both *Seinfeld* and *That '70s Show* were filmed at CBS Studio Center in Studio City, Los Angeles, right next door to each other. *Seinfeld* aired on NBC, and *That '70s Show* aired on the Fox network.

Each morning, for the remainder of that spring, Jerry Seinfeld and I arrived at CBS Studio Center about the same time. He was friendly in person and sometimes offered me a wave as he headed in the door, although I was scared as shit to talk to him. I still felt a stigma about my heavy accent, and even though my character had a heavy accent, too, I was still trying to reconcile the facts about my origins and identity with where I was now. For so long, people had told me in subtle and not-so-subtle ways that if you have an accent, you must be stupid. It was a lie straight from the pit, of course, but I was still trying to shake off that faulty belief system.

What made me laugh, though, were the differences in how Jerry and I got to work. For me, it was the city bus or Dad's old two-toned Ford. For Jerry, it felt like he drove a different Porsche every day. I mean, not just every day of the week. But a different Porsche each day of the *month*. I silently shook my head at that number, but inwardly I dreamed of that kind of financial stability. In the tough world of sit-coms, Jerry was on top—and I was getting closer to greatness, literally less than twenty feet sometimes. I thanked God I could make fifteen grand for the pilot.

The pilot turned out to be a hit, and our show was picked up for the first season. We did a show about Eric's birthday, and another about streaking, and another about Eric landing a job at a burger joint. There were a lot of laughs, and a surprising amount of heart. The car Eric drove, a dented and dinged 1969 Oldsmobile Vista Cruiser, soon morphed into a TV icon, with all of us kids shown riding in the station wagon with heavy rock music blaring during the show's opening sequence.

The fall of 1998 began, and I started my senior year at Taft. Once the show began airing regularly, I assumed I'd become the new cool guy in school, but I was dead wrong. The hairdo I had on the show wasn't the same as how I did my hair normally. I wore groovy threads on the show, which wasn't what kids my age wore in everyday life. And, you know, kids can be kids. So I got a lot of questions from my classmates, but few were complimentary. The question, "Is that really you on TV?" was probably the kindest. I also received, "Why do you talk like that?" "Why do you sound so stupid?" "Why do you look so ugly on the show?" and "Why aren't you the cute one?"

Some of my teachers watched the premiere and congratulated me. But as the fall wore on and winter began, other teachers began to grumble that I certainly wasn't in class much. Word got back to me, and I felt sad, because I thought we had worked it all out. A couple of teachers wanted to fail me, and a couple of others started saying I shouldn't be allowed to graduate—even though I was still doing my homework, turning in all assignments, and getting good grades on tests. Strangely, although I had done a lot of school plays in earlier years, and I'd loved drama class, when I got a part on a sitcom, it seemed to me that the same drama teacher wanted to fail me. I couldn't understand why she felt that way. I respected her so much.

Fortunately, a different teacher, Edwin Tucker, really stuck his hand in the fire for me. He taught government, US history, and economics, which were also some of my most favorite classes. Mr. Tucker was a tall, well-dressed Black man with a bald head and glasses who looked and sounded like a cross between Samuel L. Jackson and Malcolm X. He wore dress shirts and slacks with suspenders every day, and he carried a cane, just for the distinguished look. He would walk into a classroom and exclaim, "Oh, praise the Lord! Who's here to learn today?" I sat at the front of his classes and raised my hand for nearly every question he asked.

Mr. Tucker had met me a few years earlier when my English was horrible, and he'd taken the time to ask me about my story, about coming to America and my family's struggles and needing to learn English. When he found out that I was playing a character on a TV show, he was so proud and supportive of me. He held a meeting with the rest of my teachers and helped cast a wider vision for them. I wasn't present at the meeting, but I heard about it in detail afterward.

"What are you guys doing?" he'd asked. "You want to hold back this young man while he's living the biggest moment of his life? You have to realize that by him being on this show, he's not only changing his life, but his entire family's lives too. I tell you, if this kid were white, you'd rename the school after him. But you guys want to fail him for attendance?!"

Apparently, you could hear a pin drop. I owe Mr. Tucker a great deal, because after his meeting with the other teachers, the problem was resolved. Besides changing the other teachers' minds, his confidence and belief in me gave me the fuel to know I was on the right track. Somebody believed in me besides my mom and dad and sisters. It helped deepen my resolve to do a great job. People had sacrificed for me. I could see farther and dream deeply with confidence because I stood on the shoulders of giants. I couldn't let them down.

When I finished my senior year, my grades were solid, and Mr. Tucker made a specific point of telling me to invite my costars, the producers, and writers to my high school graduation. Many people from the show came. There was Ashton, Topher, Mila, Danny, Kurtwood, and Debra Jo, along with my family, sitting on the football field, watching me walk across the stage and receive my diploma. I walked off the stage, found my father, and handed my diploma to him.

He and I both cried.

EVERY FRIDAY NIGHT, *THAT '70S SHOW* WAS FILMED IN front of a live studio audience of 325 people. It was a big adrenaline rush every week, and I soon discovered I loved the intensity and energy that came with a live audience. We shot on actual film, and film is expensive, so the pressure was on us to get our lines right the first time. We needed a lot of rehearsal time at the start, and often I came home late from the set. As we got used to each other, our rehearsal times lessened.

Topher played the straight man, the anchor of the show. His character, Eric, was afraid to break the rules, and he was a bit dorky. Eric's friends hung out with him mostly because he had a cool, unsupervised basement. Yet the more I watched Topher act, the more my respect grew for him. He was truly a fantastic actor who knew how to set up a joke perfectly. Sometimes the anchor of a show doesn't get any funny lines. Only the larger-than-life characters are given the punch lines to say. But Topher reached the point where he could make anything funny, even the setups. He was likable and relatable in real life, and his timing as an actor was flawless.

Outside of the show, Topher and I bonded quickly over mostly nerdy things. We both loved bowling, playing board games, the movie *Back to the Future*, and going to Jerry's Famous Deli on Beverly Boulevard after we were finished for the evening, where we'd eat chicken tenders with ranch dressing. I'd order lemonade, and he'd order water, because that's all he drank. He became a good friend. Once, later, he invited me to travel with him to Connecticut to hang out with his family. His folks were supersmart, beautiful people, and so kind.

Laura was playing Donna, the cute redheaded girl next door. The premise was that she was way too hot to be hanging out with any of us (which was true in real life too). But her character had charming flaws and quirkiness. Her dad, played by Don Stark, was this bumbling Italian guy with a fuzzy perm, gold chain, and 1970s jumpsuit. And her mother, played by Tanya Roberts, was a blonde bombshell/home-maker trying to find her way in life. Don has an extensive background in theater, dance, bodybuilding, and martial arts, and he played his character perfectly. Tanya was an animal rights activist and an excellent actor. She'd appeared in the last season of the *Charlie's Angels* TV show, starred in the hit superhero film *Sheena*, and played a Bond girl in *A View to a Kill*.

Laura became like a sister to me. We had a beautiful connection. For fun, we'd try to make each other laugh on set. Sometimes, in later seasons, we'd both get to giggling so hard we'd have to run to the bathroom to pee; it was just too difficult to contain. The fabulous David Trainer, who directed every episode of the show except the pilot, sometimes made us sit on opposite sides of the room because we were such cutups.

Kurtwood played Eric's dad, Red Forman, and Debra Jo played his mom, Kitty. Both in real life and on the show, they had the daunting task of molding a bunch of cave-dwelling teenagers into solid citizens. They were great mother and father figures off the set as well as on.

The character of Red had fought in the US Navy during the World War II battles of Guadalcanal, Okinawa, and Iwo Jima, and later he'd fought in Korea, so his character was patriotic, political, and tough. He liked hunting and fishing and he was convinced the younger generation was soft. Often, he called his son "dumbass," and he made a series of "my-foot-in-your-ass" threats against any character who annoyed him. In real life, Kurtwood was easygoing, brilliant, and ever so cool. He could deliver any line like ice water, and he could keep a stone-cold face while uttering the most hilarious lines, even when the cast had broken up laughing all around him. As an actor, I wanted to be as cool and flawless as Kurtwood.

Kitty was your everyday mom of the 1970s who loved cooking, hosting guests in her home, and gossiping. As an actor, Debra Jo could make any environment funny. She relied on her laugh to wrap up jokes with a bow, which was brilliant.

The character of Hyde was suspicious, street smart, and sarcastic and often discussed conspiracy theories—*the government is out to get you*, that type of thing. Danny looked effortless in his acting technique. He didn't move around a set or rely on actions to deliver his lines. Most of his jokes were made as he slouched in a chair. Hyde became a crowd favorite with fans, and he could deliver jokes off the cuff that were superb.

Ashton played Kelso, the naive jock who's first to open his mouth and first to be wrong. Ashton was far more intelligent in real life than the character he played, and he was far more serious about the craft of acting than it appeared. He always came to set extremely prepared, just like I did, and he and I soon developed a friendly rivalry to see who could get the biggest laughs from the audience on the first take.

I have to explain that whenever an audience hears a joke for the first time, the laugh is always bigger. If you mess up on the first take and try for a huge laugh on the second, the joke never lands as powerfully. If you need to do a third or fourth take, you might as well forget it. So you want to absolutely kill it on the first. Now, even if you get it right on the first take, the director will do a second take anyway, just to have a safety or a second camera angle. So Ashton and I would call ourselves the "two-takers"—meaning we'd always try to land the first perfectly, then do the second take just for fun.

Maybe the comedy competition between us wasn't completely fair. Ashton could be hilarious, but my character was genetically created to produce laughs. I could get a response from the audience just by contorting my face, and I used my character's absurdities like a weapon. Ashton did too. So I guess we'll never know for sure who won.

Mila's character, Jackie Burkhart, was self-absorbed, wealthy, controlling, and privileged. In the pilot, she was established as Donna's best friend and Kelso's girlfriend, but as the series unfolded she and Kelso had an on-again, off-again relationship. Eventually, Jackie dated Hyde, and much later, Fez. She was popular at school, a cheerleader, and always dressed in cute clothes.

In real life, Mila was nothing like her character, except for being popular. She was a lovely person—honest, intelligent, kind, and straightforward, never manipulative. She was learning Spanish in school, and she was so good she could even communicate with my mother. Marilyn often visited the set, and she and Mila became great friends. I absolutely adore Mila, and we will be lifelong friends, like brother and sister.

OUR SHOW WAS GIVEN AN ABSOLUTE GIFT. *THAT '70S Show* debuted on Sundays at 8:30 p.m., right between two huge hits, *The Simpsons* and *The X-Files*. We couldn't have asked for a better time slot; it was the biggest night on TV at the time. But our show didn't become a hit overnight, and a lot of controversy bubbled around the show in the early years.

The producers of *The X-Files* didn't like us because our rating started out too low. They didn't think we were giving them a strong enough lead-in. And our writers were constantly trying to push the envelope in what we could say and do. Many of the teenage characters on the show smoked, drank, and had sex. Soon, the show developed a reputation for being edgy and raw. Some of America was ready to hear what the show had to say, and some of America wasn't.

The infamous "circle" became a continual discussion point with critics. Basically, all the teens sat in a circle in the Formans' basement, told jokes, and talked about whatever. The room was always smoky, and we never confirmed if something was actually burning or not. We just kept the audience guessing. For our show to be on prime time and insinuate that teens were smoking "something"—this was something no network TV show had ever done before. But I think it was one reason that teens bonded so hard with the show. The issue wasn't really about smoking "something." The larger point was that teens were being teens. This wasn't a squeaky-clean show like *The Brady Bunch* or *Leave It to Beaver*. It showed teens experimenting with life's edgier side, making mistakes, and learning from their mistakes. Can anyone actually say they were completely squeaky-clean in their teen years? So there was reality to it, even within the comedy. The show built bridges between kids and their parents. "Hey, Dad, did you ever do that when you were a teen?"

Shooting the circle scenes required some innovative camera techniques. They'd put a camera guy in the middle of us with a tripod that swiveled 360 degrees. As the tripod spun, the camera person would travel from character to character really fast. As an actor, you had to wait a split second when the camera came to you, then deliver your line spot-on—and all the way from Jupiter. It all went superfast and seamlessly, and director David Trainer taught us to not let a laugh die down before we started the next joke. David was one of the best mentors I could have asked for early in my career. He shaped me as an actor, day in and day out, season after season. It got to where he could trust us all to deliver. He was serious about the craft, but he also let us have fun on set, never forgetting we were in the business of getting laughs.

The show was often innocent and sweet too. The characters all got along, and the bulk of the smiles that characters had for each other on-screen were genuine off-screen as well. None of us ever took the show for granted. We stayed humble in real life, even though over time we began to live larger when work was done for the day. Each week, probably until season six, we worried that we were going to get canceled on the spot. But we kept coming back, week after week, performing our hearts out.

It seemed the more we bonded in real life and bullshitted between takes, the funnier the show became. The moments between the scenes drove the energy that went onto film. We laughed. We joked. We pranked each other. A rich camaraderie emerged between cast members. We'd show up to each other's rehearsals and scenes just to watch, even if we didn't have to be there. As costars, we became each other's number one fans. We had all come in so green. But after a couple of seasons, we became airtight, able to consistently create the biggest roars of laughter from each week's live audience.

Our pranks on set were all slapstick. I mean, this was junior high summer camp stuff. We crouched in closets so we could jump out and scare each other. We lay silently under beds, sometimes for up to half an hour, only to grab someone's legs when a scene began. We hid in the back seats of each other's real-life cars, only to jump up when the person slid into the driver's seat and say, "Hey, would you mind dropping me off at Jerry's Deli?"

Eventually, the taping of *That '70s Show* became the place to be. In time, it seemed like all of Hollywood stopped by on Friday nights and became our friends. Famous actors sat in the audience, laughing their heads off. Bruce Willis. Mark Hamill. Anne Hathaway. Jessica Simpson. Katherine Heigl. Erika Christensen. Afterward, we all hung out and enjoyed drinks, dessert, and music in our dressing rooms. The backstage of *That '70s Show* became the place to be. Mila had started the series with two dressing rooms, because one was for her school-work. But she soon announced she didn't need all the space, so we set up a secret craps table in the extra room and played craps each Friday night after the show.

As the show became larger, other famous actors began to do guest appearances. I can't remember everybody, but the list became long and the names were huge. Tommy Chong became a recurring character and a fan favorite, appearing in sixty-five episodes. Brooke Shields was on for seven episodes. Dwayne "The Rock" Johnson made a cameo. Don Knotts. Luke Wilson. Jim Gaffigan. Morgan Fairchild. Bobcat Goldthwait. Dick Van Patten. The incredible Betty White. The legendary Mary Tyler Moore. Marion Ross and Tom Bosley from *Happy Days*. Tom Poston from *Newhart*. Howard Hesseman from *WKRP in Cincinnati*. Shirley Jones and Danny Bonaduce from *The Partridge Family*. Gavin MacLeod from *The Love Boat*. Barry Williams, Eve Plumb, and Christopher Knight from *The Brady Bunch*. Musicians Alice Cooper, Paul Anka, Ted Nugent, and Roger Daltrey from The Who. It was incredible to meet these legends.

In spite of all the extras on set, we stayed close as a cast. We often hung out after work and ate dinner together. We traveled on promotional tours and spent hours with each other on buses and in airports. Sometimes it seemed like we spent more time with our cast family than with our real-life families. But I never forgot where I came from.

By the end of season one, as I was ready to graduate from high school, I had appeared in twenty-five episodes, including the pilot; and I had pocketed, before agency fees and taxes, $255,000. Mom and Dad were speechless. The next season, the agents negotiated slightly better pay for us, and the pay just kept going up, year after year. We were incredibly blessed. I moved my family from our two-bedroom rental into a somewhat bigger rental. And I'll never forget the day when I was able to buy my family a house of our own. The house wasn't big, but we moved into a place my parents were proud of again. A few negotiations later, I made plenty more. I was twenty years old. I didn't own forty-six Porsches, but I bought myself a 1999 Cougar to be my daily commuter. No more bus. Season after season, our show kept getting renewed. Our ratings were consistently solid. At its peak, ten to twelve million people watched *That '70s Show* every week. Soon, my finances were such that my mother and father never had to worry about food or a roof again. As a family, we started taking vacations, experiencing new things we couldn't have even imagined. Dad never drove a Lincoln Continental again, but soon I bought him a big four-door BMW sedan.

The years flew by. It seemed like I blinked and it was season three. I blinked again, and it was season five. I blinked again, and we'd done eight seasons. I was nominated five times for the American Latino Media Arts Award for Outstanding Actor, and I won the Teen Choice Award for Actor or Sidekick three times. The show was nominated twice for the People's Choice Awards for Favorite Television Comedy. The costumes were so dead-on that our department won a Primetime Emmy. Our show was nominated for fifteen other Emmys and a host of other awards.

After a series of successful contract negotiations, my life—and the life of my family—had completely changed. In season eight, when I was twenty-five, I bought Chuck Norris's home in California. It needed some renovations, but I wasn't worried. By then, we were some of the highest-paid actors on television. We weren't Jerry Seinfeld rich. Or rich like the cast of *Friends*. But we were all doing very well. I'd gone from rags to riches, from eating ninety-nine-cent pizzas to making investments and buying businesses. How could that happen? Only in America.

SOMETIMES I READ POP CULTURE SITES TODAY THAT try to analyze *That '70s Show*. Our audiences and critics alike stuck by the show during its run, so I never heard much negative feedback when we were on the air. These days, we hear a bit. Times have changed, and some of the jokes that pushed boundaries back then wouldn't work on TV now. That's okay. Eras change, and so do our perspectives as we all continue to grow.

Even so, I believe the show has a timeless quality running through it. *That '70s Show* helps a person navigate the awkwardness of the teenage years. It invites people to relive either their most embarrassing or triumphant moments. Ultimately, it shows a lightness of life where you can heal from your wounds, reflect on your experiences, or just laugh about life. That's what the show does best.

As the seasons rolled forward, we knew our characters were growing up, so we had to grow up with our characters. We couldn't stay teenagers forever. I never wanted my character to get old or feel expired, so every year I had a conversation with the writers and producers: What more do we want Fez to do? Over time, I built Fez from a character with only a few lines per episode to a full leading character.

Let's face it: the character Fez was always about comedy. But I found I could evolve as an actor by singing, dancing, and doing more scenes. And I evolved in real life. I was eighteen when we started and twenty-six when we finished. I worked out and gained muscle. I learned English perfectly. I made some mistakes but learned about life along the way.

At some point as cast members, I think we all grew tired. After eight seasons and twenty-five shows per season, we'd done two hundred episodes total. Probably during the last two years of the show, the fatigue started to set in. Topher and Ashton had left the show by then. We talked about doing spin-offs, but people felt they had done their time. Fez was the character that had jump-started my career, and I was proud of this character, despite his zany ways. I'd been in every episode, helping to create larger conversations, working to service scene after scene. But ultimately it became important to close this chapter of our lives and move forward.

On the last Friday evening in 2006 when we finished shooting the final episode, I looked out at the audience. I think we all thought we'd be ready to leave. But we weren't. Audience members were crying. Crew members were crying. We all started crying. Eventually the audience filed out, and we applauded them. They'd been so important to the show's success. But as a cast, we didn't want to leave yet. Crew members started to break down the sets, the kitchen, the living room, the basement. Another show would take our place in the same studio the next day. Normally, we'd be done by 10:30 p.m. But that night, after the work was finished, we stayed until four in the morning. Crew members, cast members, writers, producers. Everybody was telling stories, laughing, crying, hugging, saying our goodbyes. For the next ten days in a row, we all went to lunch together.

The producers invited us to take props from the show. Topher snatched the round table. Ashton got the Packers helmet. I snagged the Vista Cruiser for five hundred bucks. It didn't run. But today it still sits proudly in my garage as an icon of an era. With *That '70s Show*, we had made so many people laugh. I'd lived my dream at the highest level and was able to bring joy to so many people. It's an honor I don't take lightly, and I'll forever be thankful for my time on *That '70s Show*.

CHAPTER 6

Big Dreams, Arriving Exhausted

As an actor, you want to dream big. You want to aim for greatness. To get there, you must give a lot of yourself. Your heart can't stop beating with your ambition. Sometimes it feels like you're sacrificing pieces of yourself to achieve the dream.

Here's the catch: thousands of people have the same dream. They want it just as bad, and they're willing to work just as hard. The field is so competitive, and everybody is trying to break in, or climb to the top, or stay on top, or launch a comeback. Acting isn't for the timid. You can't succeed unless you're willing to open a vein and bleed. The trouble is, you bleed and bleed, and after that you need to bleed some more. Rejection becomes part of your life, and you have to develop a really thick skin. Only over time do you realize how dangerous this is. When you first start bleeding, you don't know the toll it will take. It just feels like a big party. I was a wide-eyed kid from Venezuela at the biggest party of my life, ready to give my soul. I still couldn't believe I'd made it through that door. I had little idea what it took to stay on the party list.

Back in my first season of working on *That '70s Show*, I started meeting all these iconic actors. I admired them so much. But I also saw how life could turn into a kind of hell for an actor who does one role for a long time and gets stuck. Success is a tightrope. It's delicate. You want your character to be memorable, but you don't want your character to consume your career or to become the only thing you're remembered for.

My agent, Shani Rosenzweig at United Talent Agency, had the foresight to know we had some work to do. We had a lot of discussions about the need for my career to continue to evolve. We both liked Fez as a character, but we both knew I had many more roles in me, and I confessed to Shani my fear of being Fez forever. I'd be one of those pop culture casualties who finishes a hit show, gets typecast, blows through all his money, and is never given the opportunity to live his art again. I had to stay alive. As strange as the timeline might sound, as early as the second season of *That '70s Show*, I began to prepare for life when the show was over.

I loved TV, and I was super thankful to be on a hit show. But I dreamed of doing more. Breaking into the movies was easier said than done. Back in the '90s and early 2000s, TV actors didn't cross over to the movies much. Not like they do today. A young Tom Hanks was one of the few exceptions. He'd gone from *Bosom Buddies* to *Splash* and *Sleepless in Seattle*. Michael J. Fox had starred in *Family Ties*, then soared with the *Back to the Future* franchise. Bruce Willis had gone on from *Moonlighting* to become a big movie star. Will Smith could do anything. Sing. Rap. Dance. TV. Movies. You name it. But he was Will Smith. That was pretty much the total list.

All at once, it seemed like all the actors of my generation were in this same discussion. Why not us? Our contemporaries, the cast of *Freaks and Geeks*, were starting to break into movies. So were the actors from *Dawson's Creek*. On *That '70s Show*, our fan base started to blow through the roof. We were versatile and multitalented, capable of playing a large variety of characters. We just needed a shot. Ashton landed parts in *Coming Soon*, *Down to You*, and *Reindeer Games*. Mila appeared in *Krippendorf's Tribe* and *Milo*. Topher started out in *Traffic* and *Ocean's Eleven*. But nothing emerged for me, not even anything small.

Shani had the smart idea for me to show industry insiders what I could do, even if there were no roles for me at the moment. "We just have to get you out there," she said. I owe so much to her care and belief in me. She began to set up meetings with every producer and showrunner she knew, having me do table reads for major studios. She wanted me in front of the insiders, so when a suitable role came up, they would remember who I was.

I began to take meetings, one by one. Meeting after meeting. Table read after table read. The schedule was an uphill climb, and sometimes a fight with producers even to get me in the room. Whenever I got into these meetings, I'd do anything not to look and sound like Fez. I'd wear a nice jacket and slacks with my hair stylishly coiffed with gel. I didn't talk in my Fez accent. I smiled professionally but didn't crack a bunch of goofy jokes. Once I was inside the door and reading, the reaction I got was like, "Whoa, who is this guy? You aren't Fez!" They could see that it had taken skill and intelligence to invent and play Fez, and if I could transform into a character so different from who I really am, then I could play anybody. Shani stayed bullish and kept introducing me all over town. I had youth and energy on my side, not to mention a terrific agent, and I wasn't content to warm the bench.

Finally in 2000, I got my chance to audition for a baseball rom-com called *Summer Catch*. I read well and landed the part of Mickey Dominguez, a young ballplayer with an accent who comes to the United States from Latin America to play ball. The more wide-eyed and naive I could play him, the better, said the producers. No problem.

I flew to North Carolina where the filming was to take place. To

my surprise, they handed me a baseball mitt, pointed to a grassy dia-
mond they'd made specifically for the movie, and told me to run out
to left field. Each morning for two months we played baseball in the
warm summer sunshine, preparing for the shoot. The whole cast was
there: Freddie Prinze Jr., Jessica Biel, Fred Ward, Matthew Lillard,
Christian Kane, Brittany Murphy, Marc Lucas, and others. In the
afternoons we rehearsed our lines and jelled as a team. I felt good
about playing baseball all summer, but this was my film debut, and I
had a thousand questions. Freddie was as helpful as could be. Jessica,
kind and beautiful, turned into another sister for me. We had a lot of
good talks. Matthew, Christian, and Marc really took me under their
wings. The other actors and ballplayers accepted me immediately and
were super helpful. I'll never forget the honor of working with Brittany
Murphy, who forever will be a sister of mine.

My character was ripped from the headlines of real life. When
young ballplayers come to town for these summer leagues, they're
often billeted with host families. Usually, there aren't any problems.
But the script called for the heat to be turned up. My host mother was
played by the legendary Beverly D'Angelo, whose character developed
a reputation for ushering young men into manhood. After the scene
was shot, the running joke was that I'd lost my on-screen virginity to
Clark Griswold's wife, which is surely the most iconic thing you could
say about any actor who came of age in my era.

In actuality, Beverly was amazing to work with—beautiful, tal-
ented, and wonderful. In addition to her roles as Mrs. Griswold in the
National Lampoon's Vacation films, she was a serious-minded Golden
Globe–nominated actor who had played Patsy Cline in *Coal Miner's
Daughter* and Stella Kowalski in *A Streetcar Named Desire*. I count it
a high privilege to have worked with her.

When the summer was over and I flew home to Los Angeles, I
reflected on my time working on my first movie. The cast had bonded

quickly. The atmosphere on set had been focused and fun. The producers and director had loved my acting. And I'd played a character who wasn't Fez.

I can do this, I thought. *This movie stuff is really going to happen.*

The entire cast of *That '70s Show* came to the premiere with me, just to say well done.

MOVIE OFFERS TRICKLED IN AFTER THAT, BUT IT WAS no flood. Somebody wanted me to play a naive foreigner with an accent, but my agent and I turned that down. Somebody else wanted me to play (big surprise) . . . a naive foreigner with an accent. We turned that down too. We didn't want me to play the same character each time.

I dreamed of becoming a chameleonlike actor, shape-shifting and disappearing into roles, hoping not to get recognized on the big screen. My friends told me that sounded weird, the opposite of what careers looked like then. But I wanted to inhabit my characters so convincingly that afterward my friends would ask, "You were in that movie? Where? I didn't see you." To me, that spelled success.

I read script after script, hunting for the perfect next roles, but they weren't easy to find—particularly ones that clicked with me and also meshed with how producers saw me. To make matters more difficult, I could only work on movies during summers when we took a break from filming *That '70s Show.* At least, that's what I told myself at first.

In 2002, I auditioned for the part of DJ Keoki in the independent biographical crime drama *Party Monster,* a movie far more serious than the title might suggest. It was a powerful, artistic script that showcased the dangers of addictions, based on the true story of a club promoter who'd allegedly killed his drug dealer. I landed the part and flew to New York. The lead character was played by Macaulay Culkin, who's about my age. I found him to be a good guy, softspoken and fun, and a tremendous actor. He'd become a megastar as a child for his work in *Richie Rich*, *My Girl*, and the *Home Alone* Christmas comedy franchise, but now he was branching out into more serious adult acting. The multitalented Chloë Sevigny, who'd been nominated for an Oscar for her work in *Boys Don't Cry*, was also in it, along with Seth Green (who was my guardian angel during the filming) Dylan McDermott, Wilson Cruz, Diana Scarwid, Natasha Lyonne, and Marilyn Manson.

Party Monster was made on a shoestring budget. We ate Big Macs and french fries for lunch. None of us had our own trailers. They strung bedsheets from one wall to another for our dressing rooms, and our sets were raggedy warehouses where you'd often see a cockroach run up the wall. Sometimes, we shot at night, maybe until five in the morning, and we didn't go to bed until 8:00 a.m., then slept until the sun grew hot. I didn't care about the conditions. I just thought, *Okay, so this is what real actors do.*

I couldn't believe it when I heard the movie would premiere at Robert Redford's Sundance Film Festival. It's a very prestigious event where independent filmmakers can get their big break. We all flew to Utah and took in the sights. Walking the streets of the festival with all these remarkable young actors felt dramatic and weird all at once. I was one of them. The young stars. None of us had done this movie for the money. We did it because it was good art, and we believed in good art.

Later, *Party Monster* was shown overseas at Cannes, arguably the most notable film festival in the industry, although I wasn't able to make the trip. Audiences applauded the movie, and we heard it was one of the most talked-about films that year at Cannes. Despite the positive reception, it was considered too dark a movie for mainstream acceptance and didn't do much at the box office. But I shrugged that off. Surely, I was on my way forward and up.

The next summer I deliberately did something different. I voiced the role of Rodrigo, a bighearted Chihuahua in the animated children's movie *Clifford's Really Big Movie*, based off the characters from the classic book *Clifford the Big Red Dog*. I love animation, and I'd always wanted to play a cartoon character. Looking back, it might have been stereotypical for me as a Latino to play a Chihuahua, but it made sense at the time. Roles for Latino actors in animated movies didn't come up often. These were the days before *Encanto*.

In 2005, a friend, Bille Woodruff, was directing a comedy called *Beauty Shop*, a spin-off of the *Barbershop* film franchise. He called me up and was like, "Would you rather have a cameo with Queen Latifah or Kevin Bacon?"

"Queen Latifah is the bomb," I said. "But if I have to choose, I'll pick Kevin." There's this old party game called "Six Degrees of Kevin Bacon," and now I could be one degree away in real life.

Being in that movie felt so surreal. Kevin's character, Jorge Christophe, is this beauty shop guru who ends up washing my character's hair. In between takes, Kevin told me he was a big fan of *That '70s Show* and we even joked that he'd modeled a few of his character's mannerisms off Fez. We had a good conversation, and I had to pinch myself. I'd reached new heights. In the history of the universe, how many people can actually say they've had their hair shampooed by Kevin Bacon?

I WANTED TO HAVE A HAND IN A MOVIE THAT COULD deeply impact society. The opportunity came along in 2005, with about a year to go of *That '70s Show*. Journalist Eric Schlosser had written a book called *Fast Food Nation* that investigated the fast-food industry, examining everything from the slaughterhouses and meat-packing plants to the restaurants that churn out artificially flavored burgers and TV commercials directed at kids. What he found wasn't encouraging, and his goal was to create an exposé on film where he basically said, "Look, people, do you realize this crap is going on?!"

Film director Richard Linklater teamed with Eric to create a movie based on the book. It wasn't a documentary. They created a fictional series of stories in one movie that intertwined and showcased the themes of the book—namely, how tyrannical the fast-food industry could be.

One of the stories featured a young couple stealing across the border from Mexico into the United States, heading for Colorado in hopes of finding jobs in a slaughterhouse. Strangely, I auditioned for the role of Raul in English, knowing full well it was going to be a Spanish-speaking part. I landed it. Catalina Sandino Moreno played Sylvia, my wife. Ana Claudia Talancón played her sister, Coco, who also travels with us. My character, Raul, gets hurt on the job, and our storyline shows the injustices that can happen to families if they don't speak English or have money. The movie also shows the reality of desperate border crossings, how parents sometimes cross borders first in search of livable wages, then send for their children, who must travel by themselves, sometimes as young as eight or nine years old. In other storylines, the movie featured a parade of iconic actors, including Kris Kristofferson, Greg Kinnear, Patricia Arquette, Ethan Hawke, Avril Lavigne, Luis Guzmán, Paul Dano, Bruce Willis, and more.

Fast Food Nation was shot in an edgy guerrilla style, and it premiered at the 2006 Cannes Film Festival. I flew to Cannes this time, and it was an amazing black-tie affair complete with yachts and royalty, everything you could ever imagine. But the feeling that struck me deepest was complicated. There I was, standing on the red carpet, and I had what can only be described as "a moment." I'd come so far from my days of scrounging for enough change so my family could get a ninety-nine-cent pizza. But I felt weird. Like nothing I'd ever experienced. I felt ecstatic and happy and anxious and driven—all at the same moment. So much was going on just then, and I didn't know what was next.

TO EXPLAIN: SIMULTANEOUSLY, WHILE I WAS WORKING on movies during summers off from *That '70s Show*, I began exploring parts in other TV shows too. Those experiences culminated at Cannes in 2006.

Back in 2002, I was invited by friends to guest star on the TV shows *Grounded for Life* and *MADtv*. Everything was fun, and it was a very fruitful time. Right around that same time, Ashton Kutcher approached MTV and created *Punk'd*, a hidden-camera reality TV show where he played practical jokes on all his buddies and a whole circle of others. I was featured in three episodes of *Punk'd*, met a lot of people from MTV, and ended up helping Ashton book our friends for the show. (Afterward, those friends stopped accepting my invitations to dinner.) I saw how much Ashton loved producing, so I was inspired to do it too.

Creating a show for MTV required a larger thought process. The television industry had its own hierarchy back then, and if you acted in a show on prime-time network TV, then you didn't do stuff on cable TV, because conventional wisdom said there wasn't any money in cable, plus the content wasn't considered "proven." But Ashton and I didn't give a shit. We talked between ourselves and concluded that opportunity was opportunity. We liked MTV, because MTV connected with our generation, and we both were frequently doing promos on MTV's show *Total Request Live* (known mostly as *TRL*). All I needed now was an idea for a show. It had to be inexpensive, because

MTV wasn't shelling out much for shows back then, and it had to be fairly straightforward, because I was still working full-time on *That '70s Show*. Most of all, it had to be wildly entertaining. The show had to pique the interest of this new generation of MTV viewers, known for quickly changing the channel if something sucked.

One night I was at home flipping through channels on TV. I started out watching the movie *8 Mile*, and I saw Eminem's character rap-battling people in the underground hip-hop scene. I thought, *Oh man, that's so cool, so funny, so street.* It reminded me of my days as a kid in Venezuela. Back then, if someone insulted my mother, I'd go ballistic. But I'd since learned after coming to America that deliberately insulting someone's mother, under certain circumstances, is a credible comedic art form. The people doing the trash-talking aren't actually disrespecting each other's mothers, and the insults aren't taken personally or literally. The style is about wit and quick thinking, all with the goal of making people laugh.

The style originated from this old street game called "Dozens," or "The Dozens," which had been around for decades, where two people insulted each other, competition style, until one was declared a victor. The world's brainiest sociologists have written doctoral dissertations on The Dozens. That got me thinking. I switched channels, and my movie *Summer Catch* was on. There's a scene where two ballplayers are talking smack to each other, and one of the jokes is, "Your momma is so fat, when she wears high heels, she drills oil."

It felt like a lightbulb switched on over my head. I called my agent and said in a rush, "I've got an idea. It's so simple. I think I can create an entire show about telling 'Yo Momma' momma' jokes. People will come on the show and insult each other's mother. It'll be a good-natured smack-talk tournament, and whoever tells the best jokes will win some cash. That's the whole show. I want to pitch it to MTV. What do you think, and how do I do that?"

My agent chuckled and said, "Well, slow down, Wilmer. It's not a bad idea. But first you need to have a production company." I didn't have one, but she told me how to start one. It wasn't as hard as it sounded. The company I crafted was just me at the time, and I named it WV Productions, as basic as it comes. I had some meetings with MTV executives, and my pitch was pretty simple. I planned to travel to all the hoods in America, bring out the funniest raw talent around, and have them talk shit about each other's moms. The competition wouldn't be about humiliating the other contestant. It would be an exposé of grassroots comedy where we showcased the best original comedic art around the nation.

The MTV executives smiled, in a genuinely friendly way, and said, almost word for word, "You know, Wilmer, that's a hell of an idea. We appreciate the bare-bones production costs. There's just something about rewarding bad behavior that works."

I partnered with another production company called Evolution Film and Tape that'd done *Big Brother* and *Fear Factor*. They knew far more than me about getting a show up and running. We shot the pilot in LA, and we got picked up right away, beginning regular runs in 2006. As a host, I got together with Jason Everhart and Sam Sarpong at first to be cohosts, and later Destiny Lightsy, and our show was given the time slot right after *TRL*, which was a great spot to land. Our sets were actual parking lots and real alleyways. Kids stepped up and represented their neighborhoods, each vying to be the funniest trash-talker around. We judged on four factors that we called "originality, delivery, quickness, and sting." The show was fast-moving and rhythmic, and surprisingly filled with respect. And it was fun. Man, it was such a good time. Sometimes we put so much pressure on ourselves in these jobs that we forget to have fun. But "fun" was definitely the spirit of my show. I did it because I loved it. Actual jokes included:

Yo momma's so old, she got pregnant and had grandkids.

Yo momma's so stupid, she tripped over her cordless phone.

Yo momma's so broke, for Christmas she brought home a tape of other people opening presents.

Yo momma's so fat, you took her to show-and-tell in the third grade and never got to the telling.

Yo momma's so dumb, she called me the other day and said, "What're you doing, baby?" And I said, "Watching *That '70s Show*." She said, "Which one? *Good Times* or *CHiPs*?"

I howled at that last one. Very quickly, *Yo Momma* became a phenomenon in urban high schools and colleges across America. Apparently, teachers didn't like me much. Word got back to me that they'd walk through their schools and be upset because all they could hear was people talking smack about each other's moms. But the audience loved the show, and *Yo Momma* soon became a major hit on MTV. We aired five shows a week. Each Friday, the winners of that week's shows would duke it out. Soon enough, we had the country's hottest urban icons, musicians, and rappers appearing as celebrity judges: E-40, Method Man, Jermaine Dupri, Ne-Yo, and many others. We did a season in LA, then another in New York, then another in Atlanta. We also did East Coast versus West Coast battles. We even took versions of the show internationally. All told, we did sixty-four episodes in the United States and a bunch of others around the world.

For me personally, it felt like a strategic career move because it showed viewers that as a TV personality, I could be more than Fez. The show was cool and edgy for the era, and I'd drive onto the set in a Chevy lowrider, climb out, and finally be right in the mix of my generation. At the time, MTV was the place to be seen. *Yo Momma* became the number one afternoon show on MTV. That introduced me to a whole different demographic of viewers. People now finally knew what I looked like when I didn't have Erik Estrada hair.

On a larger level, as much as the show was about talking smack, I believe the show helped broaden the cultural landscape. It was good for us as a nation. A lot of the shows on MTV at the time featured kids from Laguna Beach who lived very privileged lifestyles. But our show featured kids who were not rich or culturally elite. They were real kids from the inner cities who were supersmart and funny and talented and powerful and beautiful. *Yo Momma* gave them a platform.

On an even larger level, it showed a younger viewership that you could solve disputes without fights and guns. Part of the appeal of *Yo Momma* was seeing how the performers kept it together after being insulted. Some of the jokes would get personal, and sometimes we'd even bring out family members to see how the contestants reacted when the people they loved were in the line of fire. But that only brought about more respect—both competitor to competitor and audience to performers. Like boxers after a fight, competitors often embraced at the end of a show. It was about performance and love and going the distance.

It's hard to describe the depth of love our fans developed for the show. Whenever I showed up in Atlanta (the show had been going for a while by then), the reception was unbelievable. Neighbors would get together and put on impromptu barbecues with the best Southern food I'd ever tasted. Everybody was invited—judges, crew, competitors. They're like, "Wilmer's here! Woo-hoo! Have a plate of food." Those were precious times in my career.

Today, so many years later, sometimes when I walk down the street, people will still stop and ask when we're going to resurrect *Yo Momma*.

My standard line, with a grin, is, "Hey, whenever your momma calls me back."

SO MY SCHEDULE WAS CRAMMED WITH HOSTING *YO Momma*, starring in *That '70s Show*, and doing movies each summer. But I found time to play roles on other TV shows. *Higglytown Heroes* was one of those fun little opportunities. My nephew, Christian, had been born by then, and we were so happy to have him join our family. He's Marilyn's child. I honor her always. My sister is a strong single mother, and we've been blessed as a family to step up, gather around her, and support her. My nephew is a dream kid—the kindest, funniest, most respectful, cool-ass kid ever. For Christian's sake I was glad to appear on a show for children. It wasn't a big part, but Christian loved it.

My friend Seth Green developed a wild stop-motion animated show for grown-ups on Adult Swim called *Robot Chicken*. It's hilarious, and it became a successful pop-culture show. Part of its appeal is that Seth knows everybody, and everybody loves him. He could basically phone any celebrity in Hollywood, and they'd appear on his show. One episode was a spoof of *That '70s Show*, and I came on and voiced Fez for it.

In 2006, I played myself on HBO's hit crime drama *The Sopranos*. Two of the lead characters are in Hollywood pitching a movie. They end up accidentally hanging out in a gifting suite, one of those hotel rooms where they give celebrities free stuff, and while there, they bump into a recognizable actor. So the producers called me up and asked me to play myself. That was flattering. *The Sopranos* was a mainstream Emmy- and Golden Globe–winning show in its sixth season by then with a huge audience, and the fact that they knew the name Wilmer Valderrama felt like a big pat on the back. Sir Ben Kingsley guest-starred in the same episode. Two years earlier, we'd done an all-star stage reading for charity of the screenplay *Sunset Boulevard* at the Pantages Theatre in Hollywood. After all, Hollywood is a really small town.

Just as *That '70s Show* was winding down, I was watching TV with my nephew one evening and noticed that a lot of the shows he loved were filled with poop and fart jokes. They were meaningless, leaving nothing of value behind. He was five by then, and I murmured, "This is the junk you're watching?" That might sound odd for a guy who'd just created *Yo Momma*, but this was my deeper side coming out, and I wondered if a show for young kids could be both entertaining and educational at the same time.

My agents and I went to Disney and discussed the idea of me doing a show for kids. They had a computer-animated children's show in development called *Handy Manny*, and they were looking for someone to voice the main character. He was a handyman, and with me in the mix, we wondered if a Latino handyman might be too stereotypical, even offensive. But I saw this character as a strong opportunity to introduce a hardworking businessman to kids who's also the hero to his community. Handy Manny can repair anything, and he shows up when he's needed—and he's proudly Latino. That all felt extremely positive.

Disney and I worked together to help broaden the character even further. He has a team of talking tools, and they all become like a family. I wanted Handy Manny to be as thoughtful as he is fun, and I wanted him to talk about culture a lot. He has a love interest, and it's a good relationship. It was the first time in Disney's history, specifically with their preschooler division, where they featured a bilingual character who seamlessly spoke English and Spanish. The show turned out to be really cool. We had the band Los Lobos perform the opening music. I had my costars from *That '70s Show* do cameos.

Just before it launched, I promoted the show like it was going to be on prime time. I started with an appearance on *Live! with Regis and Kelly*, followed by a bunch of talk shows. I did interviews in English and Spanish and told the world I was tired of seeing the mindless stuff that my nephew had been watching. Disney and I built something we could be proud of, that my nephew and other kids of his generation could love. *Handy Manny* debuted on Saturday mornings at nine, and a whopping 8.8 million people watched the first show. That's an incredible number.

Disney was ecstatic. Rich Ross, Gary Marsh, Nancy Kanter—these executives at Disney soon became mentors and friends to me. Over the next season of my life, they taught me how to think about programming, how to think about family, and how to think about what we were saying with these characters. A lifelong trust developed between us, where doors would soon open to new opportunities.

Handy Manny quickly became the biggest preschool show in Disney's history. We ran for 113 episodes, from 2006 to 2013, a huge hit.

SO THERE I WAS, CAUGHT IN THAT CRAZY MOMENT, standing on the largest red carpet in the world. I was twenty-six years old. Right when *Handy Manny* started, the movie *Fast Food Nation* also came out, and I flew to France and stood on the red carpet at Cannes next to Ethan Hawke, Patricia Arquette, Bruce Willis, Kris Kristofferson, and Catalina Sandino Moreno—all movie stars in that film. After our movie was shown, the audience gave it a nine-minute standing ovation.

That was when it all came together for me. I couldn't believe the success I was experiencing. Who was I to be on this carpet? I was the child who'd sat on my dad's lap, driving the tractor in a dusty Venezuelan field. I was the middle-school student, set back a year for his lack of language skills, who sat in the corner of the lunchroom with his sister and couldn't summon the courage to talk to anybody. I was the teenage restaurant worker who got yelled at for not knowing the English word for *water.*

Here I was at Cannes. All at the same time, *Handy Manny* was a hit preschool show on Disney, *Yo Momma* was the number one afternoon show on MTV, *That '70s Show* was a huge comedy on TV, *Fast Food Nation* had just received its nine-minute standing ovation, *Entertainment Weekly* had just done a long article on me, I was set the next year to revive the role of Ponch in a movie version of *CHiPs,* and the future looked nothing but bright. I was happy. If you could define the American dream, then it was surely characterized by my life.

Wasn't it?

I tried to envision myself in five years, and what I truly wanted was to be one of the most influential performers that the entertainment industry had ever seen. But it was a very conflicted feeling. I also felt humbled. Leveled. Because I knew I had to keep rowing the boat upstream. I might be moving smoothly for now, but it could bog down in a Hollywood moment if I let down my guard and stopped rowing. The momentum would vanish. I needed to keep proving myself, and not just once, not just for a decade, but keep proving, proving, proving.

The entirety of that feeling is so hard to describe. All these emotions swirled together within me. I realized I was living in a way that's been so aptly described as burning the candle at both ends. I had been supporting my family since I was eighteen. I stayed up late every night, going out with friends to clubs. I was up early every morning and on set, because every moment of every day was filled with work. I had developed this little dry, reoccurring cough from a cold I couldn't shake, and I had constant bags under my eyes.

My realization was this, and this was a dangerous place: everybody has a breaking point, and I'd reached mine. I had arrived, yes, but I was drained, depleted, exhausted. And now I had to keep running.

CHAPTER 7

What's the Hurry?

A group of actors and insiders is flying back to Hollywood from New Orleans after the Super Bowl, but nothing is smooth about this flight. A winter storm rages across the skies, and the mood on board is shaky. We're in a small chartered plane. Colin Hanks. Ashton Kutcher. Danny Masterson. A couple of other friends and colleagues. I can't see anything through the window. Outside is nothing but darkness and sleet. The plane is pitching up, down, side to side. I'm feeling lightheaded. It's getting hard to breathe. Oxygen masks drop from the ceiling, and I wonder if they dropped because the turbulence shook them loose or if it's something else.

"Hey!" I shout to the pilot. "Should we put these on?"

He turns to us from the front seat. He's already got on a full Air Force mask, far bigger than ours, and he shouts back to us in an echoey voice that sounds like he's got a plastic cereal bowl over his mouth, "Yeah, I would."

We fumble with our masks. Something is definitely not right with this plane. Colin clutches the armrests of his seat with a death grip. Ashton's jaw has dropped to his lap. The captain explains that an oxygen valve got stuck closed, and our plane is filling with carbon monoxide.

"I can't feel my arm," Danny says through his mask.

"Weird," Ashton says.

"No, I'm serious," Danny says. "I have no feeling in my arm."

"The oxygen hose must be clogged," the captain says.

Ashton and I decide to share one mask and hand the other one to Danny. I suck in a lungful of oxygen, remove my mask, and hand it to Ashton. He takes a deep breath, then hands it back to me.

"We're gonna land!" the captain shouts.

No, this is definitely not good. Not good at all. We are still a long way from home. In a flash, I'm trying to remember what kind of geography is underneath us, wondering if we're flying over one of the many snowy mountain ranges of New Mexico. I'm struggling to imagine a best-case scenario if we crash high on a mountainside and they can't find us. Ashton's gonna wonder who to eat first. It's probably gonna be me, because he loves Latin American food. Meanwhile the captain is muttering into his headset to a control tower somewhere. The plane is descending far too quickly. Our ride grows incredibly turbulent. A potato chip bag pops due to the intense cabin pressure. Our plane is going down.

Moments later the wheels touch the tarmac, and we let out a cheer, but it feels like a lifetime has just passed. It's not a happy cheer. It's a wobbly cheer, like we're all trying to process what just happened. The plane taxis to the private terminal, and all of us are quiet, definitely spiraling our thoughts into what could have been. The plane comes to a rest. Our aircraft isn't flyable and it can't be fixed tonight. The captain announces that we've made an emergency landing in El Paso, Texas, and we'll have to wait for another plane to come pick us up so we can get back to California. But I don't care how long it takes. I'm just glad we're on the ground. The first thing I do is call my mother.

I don't tell her what happened. I don't want to worry her. All I say is, "I love you."

A few days later, the story gets picked up by a bunch of media sources, and by then it's been spun so many times that in its last telling, we were all passed out and Ashton has given us all CPR. I can confirm that didn't happen because I would have remembered his lips. Ladies, am I right?

In all seriousness, I'm still thinking about that night. It was way too close, and I keep replaying the events in my mind, wondering what might have happened if we hadn't landed safely.

THE AIRPLANE INCIDENT HAPPENED A FEW YEARS into *That '70s Show*, and I needed some space to think through questions of that depth, but I didn't have any space in my life. The thoughts hung with me for some time but didn't have a place to go. I just sat on them while I kept working and going out. After the series finale of *That '70s Show* in May 2006, it finally felt like I could breathe a little, and I began my "hiatus years," calling them that because I didn't appear every week on TV for a while, other than on *Handy Manny*. I needed to sort through what life was about. What made life worth living? What did I truly value?

I was twenty-six when the show ended, and although I was grateful for the success I'd achieved, in some strange way it felt like I'd missed out on many of the so-called normal experiences of a young adult. I'd spent so much of my late teens and twenties consumed by work, memorizing lines, showing up on sets, giving interviews with media personalities to promote projects, commuting long distances on the LA freeways, knocking on doors and taking meetings with producers and writers. I felt like I'd lost touch with people. I hadn't gone to university, but that window seemed closed for me, at least for a while. Sure, I'd been flying back from the Super Bowl in a private plane, which I knew was a privileged experience, but I didn't know what it felt like to go to a regular college football game with my fraternity friends or hang out in a student union building on campus. The way I was heading, I was going to drift farther away from those memories being possible.

Even on hiatus, and even while I was trying to process these larger questions, I decided that work in film and TV could never stop. Work was ingrained in my mindset. With the way I'd been raised, it wasn't an option for me *not* to be working. In fact, I even sped up my pace, although some activities were different. The incident in the plane didn't dampen my enthusiasm for travel, and not being on TV each week allowed me to get away even more. I felt like a free spirit for once. Traveling became my prescription to push through exhaustion. I didn't want to do less. I wanted to do *more*. My plan was to keep going until I could go no further, because I might not ever work again, and I'd never get my youth back.

I wasn't complaining about the full years I'd just had. I was immensely grateful for where I'd been and what I'd done and the opportunities that had come my way. Many of my contemporaries in their midtwenties were working entry-level jobs, trying to advance in their careers. They were hustling to make a buck so they could pay off student loans or scrape together enough cash to put a down payment on a house. I had given myself a jump start. I had gotten there before most.

So why not take a spontaneous trip? Or a few? I'm not sure exactly when these trips began. I was hanging out in a room with four or five buddies and Tadao Salima, my security detail, who's also an amazing friend, and said, "Hey, let's go somewhere. We're not doing anything for the next couple of days. Let's travel somewhere for the weekend."

My motivation was all about generosity, fun, having an adventure together, and sharing what I had built. I treat everyone like family, and I enjoyed the people I had around me. We chartered a plane and flew to Miami for a couple of days. We ate in great restaurants, hung out at the beach, shopped, saw shows, and went to clubs. The next weekend, I was like, "Hey guys, want to go to Vegas?" Off we went. The weekend after that, we drove to the airport, checked available flights, and headed for Chicago on a whim.

At first, the trips were around the United States. New York. Chicago. Dallas. Vegas. Miami. Atlanta. Austin. Then the trips started getting longer. We went international. London. Paris. Ibiza. More than once, I took a group of friends to Japan for a couple of days. I craved the adventure, the rush, the fun. Sometimes it was just Tadao and me taking a trip. I started treating myself.

The people around me were genuinely friends. It wasn't an entourage, and I wasn't just carrying along strangers. The friends who traveled with me had my back. They were working professionals with their own money. Many were actors, writers, producers, people in the entertainment business. They'd do the stuff that genuine friends do. They helped my dad bring a new TV up the steps. They helped my mom move a refrigerator. Most of the friends from that era are still my friends today.

The era of frequent, spontaneous trips stretched out for several years. Traveling became my college education. I found that the exposure to different countries and cultures helped broaden my life experiences. At times it even felt like research. Like, the more we saw, the more we knew, the better we lived. I loved talking to people overseas. Traveling made me a better performer in the sense that I connected with international audiences. *That '70s Show* and *Yo Momma* had been shown around the world, and I got recognized in every country I went to. Those trips were some of the most selfless and selfish adventures I've ever given myself. Selfless in the sense that I invited a bunch of people along. I paid for dinners and drinks and flights, just like my dad had taught me. If you have money, you don't split checks with friends. If you can pick up the tab, you do it. But the trips were selfish because every dollar I spent was to give me an unforgettable pool of perspectives. The joy was mine first, and I hoped it was theirs too. I found great joy in taking people with me on unique travel adventures.

When I was home in Hollywood, we ate at our own places. By my midtwenties I had invested in several restaurants. They'd started out as just one of those things. Ashton and I were talking one day, and we were like, "Wouldn't it be cool if we could say to people, 'Hey, come to my restaurant'?" It wasn't for bragging rights; we just thought it was cool. It was for hospitality. We love people. We love community. We weren't going to hide behind our success. Sometimes actors are like, "Oh no, paparazzi. Fans. Let's hide." But we were like, "Oh cool. You want a photo? No problem." We were real and normal, because all of us had come from real beginnings, places and seasons of life where we knew what it was like to go without. I started these restaurants so we could all celebrate together. It was kinda like I was saying, "Hey, come on over to my house, and let's share a meal together." I had a couple of places in Los Angeles. A sports bar in Hollywood. A steak house in Vegas. A couple more in Atlanta. I owned a bowling alley. Restaurants, at least those in Hollywood, last about ten years, if they're good. We were lucky that ours were. They ran their course, and then they ended. I put my money into other investments and moved on.

Wherever we went on our trips, it became a party. But not a dark party. I never did drugs, and we made sure drugs were never around. Tadao made sure of that. I was petrified to lose what I had built, and even worse, to lose myself. It was just a good-time party, and I have Tadao to thank for keeping much of the atmosphere on the ground. He became my gatekeeper, my curator of protection, my tattooed Samoan guardian angel. With him along, I always felt safe.

A couple of times we tested our luck. We went to places we probably shouldn't have, bars and parties in Long Beach or the hood. We weren't worried. I did well in the hood. These were my people, and I loved them. But somebody might drink too much, or the people hanging around us would act up, and I couldn't assume that everybody would have the same grounding that allows them to dodge the bad stuff. Somebody started talking big at a club in Miami, and a fight broke out. Tadao wrestled them apart and told them to get lost. Some stranger at a bar in New York started talking up a friend's girlfriend. Tadao told him to take a hike. When we took these trips, it's not like I sat down with everybody beforehand and went over a list of rules and regs. But if someone was out of line, Tadao was on him in a heartbeat. He'd trim the fat. None of us wanted that negative stuff around. We had nothing to prove, and we weren't confrontational people. We were there to party. To celebrate success. With Tadao's size and presence, he could enforce anything. My sister Marilyn rolled with us for some of those years, and as always, I felt protective of her. I didn't want her to be introduced to anything bad.

Usually, it was nothing but fun. We flew to New York and danced all night, and at four in the morning we ended up at some cafeteria, eating grilled cheese and tomato soup. We went to a club in Miami, and I climbed to the DJ booth, grabbed the microphone, and hyped the crowd. Everybody on the dance floor went crazy. I loved that, and so did the crowd. Again, we danced all night, and in the morning everybody went to David's Café on Lincoln Road and ate Cuban sandwiches. It wasn't like I was the most famous guy in the room. But I was on MTV, I had been on *That '70s Show*, and people often gathered around us at clubs if I sat at a table on the floor. In Hollywood, New York, Vegas, Miami, we knew many of the owners of the clubs and restaurants, and they gave us the best tables and service. Sometimes the restaurant comped us all the food and drinks. Other times, I picked up the check. The house played the music I liked, and it was all a good time.

I loved hanging with DJs. I could stay up in a DJ booth for hours. I loved spinning records and talking one-on-one with the DJs. Or grabbing a mic and turning up the night. Soon I knew all the world's best DJs—DJ Vice, DJ Steve Aoki, DJ Eric Dlux, DJ JusSke, DJ Samantha Ronson, DJ XXXL. Iconic artists, they worked their asses off to help curate the best nights that the world's biggest cities could provide. The late DJ AM used to drop his version of "Sweet Home Alabama" with a track from Run-DMC, blending the music together. It was a spectacle. That's when nightlife was really cool. We rolled up to the clubs, and the doors opened, and the DJs welcomed us to partake in the best kind of energy. That's what I loved. That's what refreshed me. That's what brought clarity to my mind.

But the nightlife started changing. It became all about getting a selfie, or seeing how many famous people a person could meet. That's what took the energy out of me. Sometimes the atmosphere could turn downright shitty. Nightlife can get that way, and a big crowd can be part of the fun. But it could get claustrophobic too. Tadao shook them loose. Or a group of people would want to sit with me because the energy was at our table—but I didn't know them and none of my friends knew them either. That felt intrusive, and it happened plenty of times. Or some guy we didn't know was inviting all his friends over, like, "Hey, come and have a drink. I'm sitting with Wilmer Valderrama," which felt fake, like the guy was showing off. Or somebody else we didn't know was pounding the free drinks at our table, and I thought, *Dude, the thirst is real.*

I'm allergic to that kind of behavior. As much as I'm an extrovert, I also like solitude, even in the midst of a party. For a couple of years, it felt like I took it on the chin. I'd been out a lot by then, and I didn't want to go out anymore, but I endured the crowded tables. I found myself often sitting with a drink in my hand, and everything seemed to move in slow motion. I'd shake hands with two hundred different strangers in the course of a night.

As time went on, I started putting better boundaries on my life. I stopped going out at night. I started going to the gym more. Then it was like boom, boom, boom, I focused on building an empire, although I had some frustrations and major letdowns too. Like, I never got to play Ponch in the movie version of *CHiPs*, a project I was so hopeful for. It could have been a level up on the road ahead for me. That project was set up in development. But in a true Hollywood twist, the movie fell apart for reasons only Hollywood and I will ever know. In the end, they ended up making a movie anyway. It wasn't the movie I would have made. It was a real disappointment for me that I didn't get to make *CHiPs*.

Do I regret one dollar spent in my hiatus years? Absolutely not. I invested in my life lessons, and I'm grateful for all of them.

YOU COME TO AMERICA FOR A BETTER LIFE, AND I HAD that better life, but I was striving to define what that better life looked like when I wasn't working. I knew how to work well, and I loved work. Work made the most sense. So I kept doing that.

After making *Fast Food Nation* in 2006, I acted in a movie called *Unaccompanied Minors*. Paul Feig had created the TV series *Freaks and Geeks*, which became a cult classic, and now he wanted to branch out into movies. I was a fan of Paul's and super excited. This was a Christmas comedy, and we flew to Utah in the winter to shoot it. Paul was a timeless director who came to the set every day in a full three-piece suit, even in the midst of a snowstorm. Sometimes we'd be shooting outside in the freezing cold, and Paul wore a puffy snowsuit. But when we went inside, he'd unzip it, and there was his three-piece suit underneath.

I respected him for that. He was a brilliant director, fun, creative, and a joy to work with. He brought a level of elegance to his work, and it showed even in the clothes he wore. It felt like we were back in old Hollywood, and it reminded me of the style my dad cultivated back in Venezuela. Paul and I bonded over his three-piece suits. Back in year two of *That '70s Show*, a bunch of us had grown enamored with old Hollywood, so we decided that every Monday and Friday we'd show up to set wearing suits as a tribute. We were only young'uns in our late teens and twenties, but we looked like old Hollywood gangsters.

My role in the supernatural thriller *El Muerto* in 2007 was also a kick. The movie was produced independently and based off a comic book. I starred in the role of Diego de la Muerte, a young man who dies on the way to the Día de los Muertos celebration, then gets resurrected by the Aztec gods. It was my first lead role, and I immersed myself in the character. The script was strong, and the possibilities seemed boundless, but halfway through production the movie ran out of money, so in the end the visual effects weren't what they needed to be. But I made some great friends and learned lots. Years later, Angie Cepeda, the woman who played my love interest in *El Muerto*, would play my wife in *Encanto*, Julieta Madrigal.

Beginning in that same year, 2007, I experienced a couple of highs and lows in the movie business. These were situations where I loved the project and worked hard, but I had no control over the end result. I voiced the lead character of Tony Valdez in the animated movie *The Condor*, where legendary director Stan Lee built a Latino superhero from scratch. Everybody had high hopes. My character, Tony, is a skateboarder and super likeable, and meeting Stan Lee and working with him was incredible.

In 2008, I played the character of Danny Boy, the villain in the indie movie *Days of Wrath*, alongside a star-studded cast of actors and rappers. The movie was about the ruthless gang wars between Black people and Latinos in East LA, and it would be difficult to say if a movie like this could even be made today, unless it was done as a period piece. Gang wars have cooled off substantially, and now it could be considered counterproductive to show Black people and Latinos at war. But back then, the movie made sense.

It was my first time to play a villain, which can be tricky. But I threw myself into the role, hoping to introduce my fans to something new. I shaved my head, grew a tough-looking beard, and had all these tattoos. Everything looked and sounded authentic. Our consultants were former gangbangers, redeemed bad dudes, and they would watch me rehearse and afterward say, "You look and sound exactly like this *vato* I knew. Damn, that fool was crazy."

To prepare, I worked out intensely and got into the best shape of my life. My character's personality was completely coldhearted. He walked around believing he was unstoppable. That was one of those roles when friends saw me during screenings, and afterward they were like, "You were in that? Where? Man, that's versatility." I took my mom to one of the screenings, and at the end of the movie my character dies in an agonizing way. She looked at her stomach and said, in this really concerned voice, "I never want to see you die again."

The movie was projected to be huge, but due to some disagreements about distribution, the director chose to shelve the project. *Days of Wrath* has never been shown in theaters or even on DVD, and today, even with all the options to view movies, nobody can see this film. You can still find the trailer online, but that's all. It's so disappointing. Sometimes you put your blood, sweat, and tears into a project only to have it fall apart. That's disheartening. I'm not sure if I've ever come to peace with it. Nothing creative is safe.

That same year, 2008, I acted in a crime drama called *Columbus Day* with Val Kilmer. Man, he's an incredible guy. So inspirational. I'd be shooting these scenes three feet away from Val, and I'd be taking notes on his technique. He could disappear so convincingly into any role. By this point in his career, he'd played Iceman in *Top Gun*, Madmartigan in *Willow*, Jim Morrison in *The Doors*, Doc Holliday in *Tombstone*, Simon Templar in *The Saint*. He'd voiced the roles of both Moses and God in *The Prince of Egypt*. And, of course, he was Batman. So much versatility. Our movie wasn't perfect, but it was a gamble we all took, and in the end I'm glad to have done it.

I was one of the four leads in the movie *From Prada to Nada* in 2011, an independent Latino romantic comedy based on an adapted version of Jane Austen's novel *Sense and Sensibility*. It's a sweet, heartfelt movie that we shot in Mexico and Los Angeles, and it became a cult classic in the Latino community.

I'd been shooting a lot of independent movies, and my business manager called one day and said, "Hey, why don't you take something that pays a little more?" I was asked to meet the producers of a prime-time TV show, more lucrative, but I passed. I didn't want to do something just for the money.

A week after I passed, I auditioned for a movie called *Larry Crowne*. I got what I thought was a callback. So I went to the studios and sat in the waiting room of this little bungalow that was going to be the production office. I glanced at the wall, and they'd already hung up the headshots of all the actors who were going to be in this movie. Tom Hanks and his wife, Rita Wilson. The incredible Julia Roberts. Bryan Cranston, who'd done a terrific job playing the father in *Malcom in the Middle* and who would later win a ton of awards in the megahit *Breaking Bad*. Cedric the Entertainer, Rami Malek, Jon

Seda, Gugu Mbatha-Raw, Pam Grier, and more. There was my photo on the wall too. I was like, *What am I doing up there? I'm only here for a callback.*

From down the hallway, I heard the unmistakable sound of Tom Hanks's voice. I couldn't see him yet, but he called out in that wonderful singsong voice he sometimes does, "Where's Wilmer? Wilmer—where are you? Where's Wilmer?" He came into view and added, "Oh, there you are. Everybody, say hi to Wilmer." I laughed.

He called me into a side room and closed the door. Just him and me. I'd brought my script and opened it, thinking he was going to do a chemistry read.

"Hey, how long did you do *That '70s Show*?" he said. "You all were very funny."

"Thanks so much," I said. "Eight years. Two hundred episodes." (*Holy shit, he's seen me on the show.*)

"You know my son Colin, right?"

"Me? Oh, I know Colin."

And off we went. The conversation flowed from there, and for the next forty-five minutes, he asked questions about my life. Where did I come from? What had I been doing lately? I was trying to answer everything as smoothly as I could. But inside my head during this whole time, I was thinking, *You're Tom Hanks. You're a cultural icon.* Tom started in television like me. Then slowly and surely, his star soared and he succeeded everywhere. Movies. Miniseries. Comedy. Drama. Producing. Directing. Writing. I thought, *I cannot believe this moment! What has my life become that I'm now sitting directly in front of my idol Tom Hanks? And Tom is talking to me like we're old friends.*

"Oh, don't worry about the script," he said, when I asked about it. "We're going to have fun on set. Whenever I yell 'Action,' we're going to see what comes out. I'm so happy you're on board."

I was like, "Wait a minute. I have the part? I thought I was just going to read for you."

"Nobody told Wilmer that he has the part?" Tom said, calling across his shoulder to an invisible audience. "Oh, that's just cruel. Yeah. Welcome aboard. You're our Dell Gordo. We gotta show you your moped."

I tried to play it cool, but inside I was like, *I can't believe this just happened.*

When shooting started, I was continually impressed with Tom—the way he treated his crew, the respect he gave people, the way he effortlessly switched between director and actor. Everybody loved being on set. I made notes for my own fledgling company, now called WV Entertainment, about the kind of energy and environment I wanted to create someday when I started producing larger projects. Tom created a wonderful sense of flow and confidence. Nothing was nerve-racking for anybody. He'd yell, "Action!" Then he'd jump into a scene and start acting. Then he'd yell, "Cut!" The scene would be perfect, and he'd call out to everybody rhetorically, like he was totally impressed, "Now, what was wrong with that, huh? Great! Checking the gates. We'll move on."

Tom Hanks mentored me in that movie, providing some of the best lessons about life and professionalism I'd ever witnessed. You could have a purposeful career and live with excellence and still have fun doing your job. Tom proved that. *Larry Crowne* ended up being a box office success, and Tom and I have stayed in touch ever since.

OKAY. IT ISN'T TOO LONG AFTER THE AIRPLANE INCI-dent. I'm still burning the candle at both ends, exhausted. This is before my hiatus years. I'm still trying to understand more about where I'm going to end up in life, and I go talk to both of my agents. (Tracey Jacobs at UTA partners with Shani Rosenzweig in heading our representative team.)

"What's next?" I ask. "What should our plan be now? I feel like we need a strategy to maximize this moment."

"Let's take a beat," Tracey says. "I want you to meet someone. Another client of mine. You'll like him."

I leave my car parked at UTA, and she drives me over to Walt Disney Studios in Burbank. I'm like, "Who am I meeting?" She says, "You'll see."

We roll up past the gates, park, and get out. In front of us are these four big soundstages with a ton of people working on a huge production. I start recognizing backdrops and props I've seen in the movies, and I'm like, "Hey, wait. Is this from—?" But before I can say the next word, Tracey says, "Exactly."

They're in the middle of shooting *Pirates of the Caribbean: Dead Man's Chest*, the second movie in the megahit franchise. Johnny Depp is at the height of his career, one of the biggest stars in Hollywood, and suddenly he walks out of one of the soundstages in full Captain Jack Sparrow mode, heading back to his trailer.

"Hey there, Tracey," he says and gives me a nod.

We follow him back to his trailer, and Tracey introduces me. We all kick back and relax. At least, I'm trying to. I can't believe I'm hanging out with Johnny Depp.

"Wilmer wants to ask you a few questions about his career," Tracey says. "You guys should chat."

We talk for a while, just about everyday things, and I say to Johnny, "I don't want to play the sidekick forever. I have *Fast Food Nation* that's just premiered at Cannes. I have the number one show on MTV. *Handy Manny* is doing great on Disney. *That '70s Show* is the number one show on Fox. I feel I need to keep the ball rolling now while things are hot, you know? If things cool down, I'm concerned that all these opportunities might end."

Johnny smiles and leans back in his chair. "Hey, Wilmer, what's the hurry?"

His whole persona communicates ease.

"Yeah," he adds. "I used to feel like that sometimes. People used to want me to play only the heartthrob. But I wanted to play all these other characters. I wanted to be Edward Scissorhands. Nobody wanted to see me as anything else. So I decided to take my time. I needed to trust myself that I was good enough to play the roles I wanted to, even though nobody saw me in those roles at first. Wilmer, you got to bet on yourself. Focus on one character at a time and you'll find yourself always working."

Johnny glances at the clock on the wall. He needs to be somewhere. We say our goodbyes. Tracey takes me back to her car.

Those deeper questions about life. I'm thinking about those questions on the ride back to UTA. I'm thinking you can answer some of them as you move. You travel. You go out. You start businesses. You work. You respect others. You hang out with lots of people over lots of years, and sometimes you make mistakes. But you learn from the mistakes and grow wiser. You work hard and have fun while you're doing it.

Tracey pulls into the UTA parking lot, stops, and motions with her chin toward my car.

"What's the hurry, Wilmer?" she says with a little grin.

I give her a hug, and she hugs me back, and I head to my car. For a moment, I sit behind the wheel before starting the engine. I'm thinking, *What if my life had ended that day on the plane?* All of us are going to die someday, and we have to prepare for what's next. But it's also important to live here and now. We have to be present in this moment, and we have to figure out how to do that. Because this moment can be so beautiful.

I'm still thinking about these things as I put my car in gear and head toward home.

CHAPTER 8

Causes to Believe In

I'm in a roomful of my heroes. Cut to a joint in my hand. *Wham.* My heart is pounding. Everybody at the gathering in the hotel suite is looking at me, and I feel a strong urge to call a Zack Morris "time-out" from *Saved by the Bell.* Usually Zack had some intense problem he needed to solve. He could magically freeze everybody around him, look into the camera, and ask for advice. That's me right now with the joint in my hand. What do I do?

Let me back up.

Two Latino actors I've always looked up to in a massive way are Anthony Quinn and Antonio Banderas. Anthony is from Mexico and incredibly talented and versatile. He played every character imaginable in the movies. And when Antonio entered the industry, he was unapologetically a foreigner. Many Latino actors are allowed to play only bad guys, and this was particularly true twenty-five years ago. But Antonio successfully crossed over and played the good guy, even while keeping his accent. He was one of the first actors who made me feel okay to have an accent and still be part of mainstream United States pop culture. I've got nothing but respect for Antonio Banderas.

So, back in the early days of *That '70s Show*, I went to Washington, DC, to be a presenter at the Hispanic Heritage Awards. I noticed that Anthony Quinn and Antonio Banderas were there. I couldn't believe I was in the same auditorium with these two idols of mine. But I presented my award, and everything went fine. After the ceremony, a bunch of people made their way to the presidential suite at a hotel for an after-party, and I got invited along. I was starstruck as hell. The world had just exploded for me.

The suite was noisy with music and packed with people. I didn't drink back then, and most everybody except me was drinking whiskey. Anthony Quinn and I had a good chat, and I couldn't believe I was at the same after-party as he was, only an arm's distance away. He soon left to go back to his room to get some sleep. I meandered over to the sitting area where a bunch of people were telling jokes and stories. They waved me in. I couldn't believe this moment either. It felt incredible.

While we were all talking and laughing, this joint started making its way around. Somehow the weed made its way into my hand.

I'm sitting there thinking, *What do I do? I've never smoked anything in my life. I've never even had weed in my hands before now. I don't want to smoke weed. (I don't even know how.) I don't want to get in trouble. But do I want to act all experienced around my idols? Should I fake it and pretend to take a hit? Should I actually try weed for the first time? I mean, if I'm ever going to try weed, this is as good a time as ever.*

Far across the room is Antonio with his intense and iconic presence. I take a pause, swallow hard, and say to the person who's passed me the joint, "Nah, I'm cool."

When I said no, nobody shamed me or looked down on me. People respected my choice.

Looking back, I see that my response said something strong about me, because as soon as the joint left my hand, that became a pivotal moment in my life. It was me realizing my strength. I'd just proved to myself that I didn't have to do anything I didn't want to do. Not then. Not now. Not ever. I was left sitting there, still telling jokes and stories, thinking about how if you muster a little strength when it's most vital, that's the moment when life alters for you. You don't need to be held down by anything. You can make your own decisions. You can be your own self. That kind of confidence can take you anywhere.

SMALL MOMENTS OF STRENGTH SHOWED UP OTHER places for me too. Not always. But they had a way of intertwining throughout my career, and when I built on those moments, I made good choices, and those choices led to other good things. I kept working in cinema, providing for my family. After *Larry Crowne* finished in 2011, and for the next few years of my hiatus, I appeared in another string of movies, including *The Brooklyn Brothers Beat the Best*, *The Girl Is in Trouble*, and *The Adderall Diaries*. They were all good experiences, and I kept meeting all sorts of incredible people.

I kept working on television too; guest appearances mostly, appearing in *Wizards of Waverly Place*, *The Cleveland Show*, *Royal Pains*, *NTSF:SD:SUV*, and *Suburgatory*. Although not all parts were guest appearances. I appeared as Detective Efrem Vega in thirteen episodes of the dreamlike police procedural *Awake*, which marked my return to TV, this time playing something my fans hadn't seen me do. It premiered well and was a hit with critics and fans alike, but its viewership numbers weren't big enough for the network to keep it, so sadly the show got canceled. That happens a lot in the world of TV. I also appeared on *Special Agent Oso*, *Are You There, Chelsea?*, and *RuPaul's Drag Race*, which I loved doing. The show is just pure magic.

I appeared as the character Ricardo Montes four times on the TV show *Raising Hope*, which was pretty funny, because my character is Melanie Griffith's love interest, and she was married to Antonio Banderas at the time. Melanie's a legend, absolutely lovely to work with. In one scene, our characters kiss. (Which I was intimidated by, because I'd seen *Desperado* so many times.)

In 2014, I guess my hiatus years were officially over, because I came back to regular TV for a good run, appearing as Carlos Madrigal for three seasons (twenty-three episodes) in the supernatural crime saga *From Dusk till Dawn: The Series*, based off a movie by Quentin Tarantino and Robert Rodriguez. The TV show expanded on the themes and characters and featured an intricate, gory plotline involving bank robbers, hijackings, vampires, and Aztec mythology. I played one of the main villains, which meant lots of gunpowder, fake blood, and fangs for me, every single night of shooting. We shot the first two seasons in Austin, then the last in New Mexico. I was getting super busy at that time, so the writers killed me after the end of season two, then brought me back to life for a couple more episodes during season three. Robert Rodriguez executive-produced and directed the show, and he was tremendous to work with. He could produce iconic badass Latino characters like nobody's business. He has uplifted the Latino community, made accents cool, and made us part of mainstream cinema. He and I are still close today.

One reason I was getting busy was that about halfway through the run of *From Dusk till Dawn*, I also started appearing as Will Blake in the futuristic crime drama *Minority Report*. I was a regular on two shows at the same time. *Minority Report* was the first time Steven Spielberg had allowed one of his movie titles to become a TV show. I appeared in all ten episodes of *Minority Report*, but it, too, was canceled after only one season.

Then came my run on *Grey's Anatomy*, the longest-running scripted prime-time show on ABC. It had been airing since 2005, and in 2016 I was called in to play the character of Kyle Diaz, a love interest of Stephanie Edwards, a surgical resident at Grey Sloan Memorial Hospital. My character is a career-level guitarist, but he's just been diagnosed with multiple sclerosis, so a hand tremor has shown up, halting his tour. The producers offered me a multi-episode arc, the character caught fire with fans, and I ended up doing five shows before Kyle developed an infection and died.

That was such a crazy time in real life, the attention my character received; I was so grateful. *Grey's Anatomy* has a huge fan base—both then and to this day. I'd be walking through an airport, and people would look at me and freak out. "We can't believe they killed you!" they'd exclaim. "We so wanted you to live!"

ANOTHER REASON MY LIFE SHIFTED INTO OVERDRIVE was that my schedule had become filled with volunteer projects, causes close to my heart. That's where an inner strength can really shine. Strangely, even though I was so busy, I didn't feel too busy, particularly when I was volunteering. I felt like I couldn't do enough. A fire had been lit inside me, a drive that kept me going, day in and day out.

Volunteering began for me in a larger way leading up to the 2004 presidential election. My friend Rosario Dawson phoned and described how too few Latinos in the United States were registered to vote. In a poll taken during the 2020 presidential election, Latinos were the second-largest voting bloc in the United States. But years ago, that wasn't the case. Additionally, many Latinos were fearful of participating in that year's national census. With language barriers and cultural differences getting in the way, some Latinos perceived the census as more of a conspiracy, worrying that the government would ask intrusive questions about a person's private life or citizenship.

Rosario wanted to assure the Latino community that a census was actually a good thing. By participating, Latinos could shape the information sent to the government so schools, hospitals, roads, and social services could receive needed funding. When it came to being registered to vote, every citizen in the United States eighteen years old and up had the right to vote. Latinos needed to show up at the polls and be counted.

Rosario, political activist María Teresa Kumar (who became a mentor to me), and several others were forming an organization called Voto Latino. They asked if I could join their first-ever census campaign. So we went to work registering voters and encouraging Latinos to participate in the upcoming census. There was little social media back then, but we ran a campaign on MTV that proved quite successful. We held street festivals and seminars, and I started traveling around the country giving speeches for the organization. I appeared at concerts and panels with artists, actors, and athletes. I started meeting with politicians, and I traveled to the White House and the United States Capitol several times. I supported the organization's grassroots efforts as well, such as talking to people when they came out of stores and encouraging them to register. And I championed some of the foundation's more difficult initiatives, such as encouraging people to vote in midterms, not just the presidential elections.

Although I hold specific political views on many issues, I personally took a nonpartisan approach to my activism, because I was more interested in educating people to vote for their interests and to vote with their hearts and minds. I wanted to empower and educate the Latino community, but I didn't want to tell them how to vote. There are a lot of countries where the people don't have the right to vote. So I encouraged people to start thinking about voting as a gift. It was a privilege to vote, just like having a driver's license is a privilege, not a right. They could help shape the landscape around them and the climate of this country, and when they voted, they helped themselves. Overall, I wanted to help create a national celebration of democracy.

Many cool results emerged from those years. I remember meeting a young Latino boy in Miami at a seminar. He was maybe eight or nine and with his parents. He came up to me afterward and asked for a photo. I said sure. We snapped a picture, and I signed an autograph for him, and we talked for a bit. I encouraged him to do his best in life, to be grateful for the opportunities his parents were providing for him, to learn to give back, and to fulfill all his potential. I remember telling him specifically, "Anything you want to do in life, you're going to do it." Years passed, and just a couple of months ago when I was in Germany on a USO tour, a young Army officer walked up to me and asked, "Remember me? I was that little kid you spoke to in Miami. You were one of the first people in the United States who told me I could do anything I wanted to do. That was incredibly impactful. I grew up wanting to serve my country, and wow, I'm doing that today, thanks in part to your inspiration." We gave each other a hug, and I had a tough time not crying. You just never know whose life you're going to impact for good.

AFTER WE FINISHED THE MOVIE *FAST FOOD NATION* IN 2006, director Richard Linklater and writer Eric Schlosser sat me down and said, "Wilmer, you have an opportunity. You have the ear of the younger generation, and you also have the ear of Washington. You have the opportunity to do some good." They were both passionate about causes they believed in, and they mentored me in the area of activism and helped me grow. They took the stance that we are given much in the United States, so much is required of us. It's up to us to do something worthwhile with the opportunities that come our way and that we create for ourselves.

The character I had played in *Fast Food Nation* was based on true stories. That's who I wanted to honor: this undocumented immigrant who crosses the border with family members, searching for a better life. He ends up working in a slaughterhouse where he gets injured and is cast aside by his employer. Where is his hope for achieving his dreams?

So I worked to understand issues thoroughly, and I kept going to Washington. Sometimes I spoke on panels alongside other leaders, actors, and activists. Other times I went alone. I spoke at congressional luncheons. I spoke on the floor of Congress. I spoke to senators. I spoke to the press. I spoke onstage at various tours, summits, and venues. Over the years, starting with Bill Clinton, I've met every sitting president except one. When President Obama was working on immigration reform, he invited me to speak on a panel and help with his initiatives. Afterward I had several meetings with him to discuss the issues closest to his heart. It was a real honor, and eventually President Obama, his staff, and I did a lot of work together on immigration reform.

We agreed that undocumented immigrants have rights too. It's far too easy for people to stand on soapboxes and shout that all undocumented workers need to be sent home. But that's clearly not the answer. Many legitimate and needful jobs are performed by undocumented immigrants in the United States. Entire industries depend on them, industries that provide goods and services that all Americans benefit from and enjoy. We wanted to help people see that immigrants can be an asset, not a problem.

One way to help is by ensuring that Latinos and other minorities are granted permission to be in the country and that they're protected and compensated while doing these jobs. We need an inclusive democracy where every person is represented and valued. We can't keep paying undocumented workers under the table or below minimum wage. If an undocumented immigrant gets hurt on the job, it's too easy for an employer to dismiss this person and ship in a new batch of workers. Part of the solution is better systems to streamline the process of documenting immigrants. They would be better protected then, and in turn they would more consistently pay federal income taxes, which would be a win-win for the country.

Years ago I met a courageous young Latina actress named Diane Guerrero. She was born in New Jersey and raised in Boston, and she'd grown up thinking that her family was American. She had American citizenship, after all. But one afternoon when she was fourteen, she came home from school and discovered an empty house. The lights were on, dinner was on the stove, and the family's car was parked outside, but her parents and older brother were nowhere to be found. Alarmed, she ran to the neighbor's house and learned that her family had been picked up by immigration agents and kicked out of the country. Diane had no idea what to do.

It turned out that Diane's parents had emigrated from Colombia before she was born. They'd escaped a dire economic climate and had come to the United States because they believed they would have a better life. For years, they held jobs in the United States. They worked hard and made a lot of sacrifices. All the while, they were trying to legalize their immigration status, but they'd been caught in a slow system. And the story gets worse. They'd hired a lawyer and paid him a lot of money, but the lawyer had run off, never to be seen again. Sadly, for her parents and brother, their time was up. They'd been deported.

It's incredible for me to think that this could happen to a fourteen-year-old in the United States. Diane was left completely alone. Fortunately, she had a caring community that helped. Even though her family had been torn away from her, she chose to stay in the United

States and pursue her dreams. Neighbors offered her a place to live. She'd been attending Boston Arts Academy, a performing-arts high school, and her principal made sure she could stay in school. Diane was able to graduate and go on to university. But her parents never returned to the United States, and she was able to see them only by traveling to Colombia.

It's stories such as those—and many others—that show how the immigration system is broken. Children should never be separated from their parents. Diane overcame her challenges and went on to have a tremendous career in acting, appearing in a long string of TV shows and movies. Today, she's best known for her roles in the hit TV shows *Orange Is the New Black* and *Jane the Virgin*. In 2021, she played my daughter, Isabela Madrigal, in *Encanto*. But I wonder how much her life could have been even better if she'd had her parents around during her teenage years.

I DON'T HOLD BACK FROM TELLING THE HARDER STO-ries, and since I do so much activism in immigration reform, sometimes people wonder what my stance is.

I'm extremely grateful for this country. This country gave me the American dream. America is not a perfect country, but it offers freedoms that aren't present in many other parts of the world. We have freedom of speech. We can gather together anytime we want. We are free to worship and practice any religion. The press are free in America to say anything they wish. America gives people the right to a fair trial. We have free public education in America, a right that isn't granted in every other country. We have the freedom to travel, vote, own property, and start businesses.

Ultimately, America offers people a chance to make something of themselves. You can achieve just about anything you want here. Instead of complaining about America, I encourage people to roll up their sleeves and be part of the solution. Even the fact that people can live in this country and critique the United States is a freedom that people in most other parts of the world don't have.

A huge four-hundred-page report called the Human Freedom Index is compiled annually by leading think tanks. It's tough and uncompromising, definitely not propagandistic in nature, using more than eighty distinct markers of personal and economic freedom to rank countries from most free to least.

In 2021, Switzerland topped the list of 165 jurisdictions scrutinized. The United States ranked fifteenth. Venezuela, where I grew up, ranked second from last.[1]

America, even with its flaws, is still a great country where freedoms abound. Don't let anybody try to convince you otherwise.

DURING MY HIATUS YEARS, I GOT TO HELP OUT WITH A lot of community leadership initiatives, after-school programs, and mentoring programs. When I worked, I was at work. When I wasn't working, I was traveling. In free hours, I devoted my time to causes that influenced people for good. I became fearless about meeting people, listening to their concerns, and speaking about the causes I believed in.

I became a spokesperson for the Congressional Hispanic Caucus Institute, an organization that develops leaders and provides educational services to young people. As part of that work, I appeared at workshops around the country, sharing my story in an effort to inspire youth to pursue their own dreams through higher education. I helped jump-start the Caucus's Ready to Lead college-readiness program, which helps Latino high school students understand their options for higher education. My dad had told me more than once to get the education he'd never had. For me, that meant completing high school. For the students I spoke with, I hoped that meant college. That was some of the most rewarding work I've ever done.

Once when I was at the White House, this young man came up to me, told me about his job working for the president, and said, "Years ago you gave a speech that really inspired me." That was a loud story, one that really rang in my ears. But I also knew that for every loud story, there are countless quieter ones. Immigrants come to America. The youth grow up. They go to college. They succeed in business. They become teachers and dentists and doctors and massive contributors to American society. Those are the quieter stories. That's who I hoped I was helping.

I started volunteering with the Christopher and Dana Reeve Foundation, which raises money to treat and cure spinal cord injuries and help support families impacted by paralysis. In 2010, I became one of their ambassadors. I hosted galas. I met people impacted by spinal injuries to hear their stories and offer support. Several times I played wheelchair basketball at the foundation's charity events. I respected Christopher Reeve so much. He had passed before I became involved, so I never got to meet him, although I met several of his family members.

Over the years, I received awards and honors for my activism. But my involvement was never about winning awards. I'd become addicted to showing up and giving back. It became a natural outflowing of my career. Like my father had taught me, when you're out with friends at a meal, you pick up the check. You give generously. And you give not only your money but your time and platform to amplify causes that matter. Responsibility and success go hand in hand, and you can't keep success to yourself. You have to pay it forward.

Following the elections of 2016, America Ferrera and I were on the phone together, and I asked how she was feeling. She was highly concerned, and so was I. It seemed as if the social climate in the United States was allowing a more hostile stance toward marginalized communities. Some Americans were misinterpreting what it meant to be free. Fringe groups were uttering frightening statements and acting with vitriol. Many minority communities were being targeted or attacked, and it felt like a license had been granted to torment and hate. I'm not sure if everyone in the United States felt that tension, but the minority communities certainly did.

We held several listening meetings, safe spaces, where people from different minority communities gathered to voice their concerns. Latinos. Asians. Black. Muslims. Native Americans. LGBTQ. We all came together. A number of people described how they had never before gathered like this, but they felt empowered to unite. The largest message we heard was that it was a vulnerable time to be a minority. They wanted to be safe and heard. They wanted to come together to reenergize, heal, and put their thoughts into action.

Soon into the new year, 2017, we cofounded an organization called Harness, along with a filmmaker, Ryan Piers Williams. We wanted to bring together leaders and communities to share their strengths and help move the needle toward restoring true freedom for all people. The foundation is still going today, running strong. Harness has become the space that welcomes the voices of the communities who are on the ground doing the work. We strive to work with marginalized communities to create a more equitable world overall in which everyone can thrive.

Our program called DEAR Hollywood strives for equal access and representation in the entertainment and arts industries. Another program called Protect the Sacred helps Native American leaders strengthen indigenous sovereignty. An initiative called Gender

Justice works to change dominant, harmful narratives around gender in popular culture. Several other initiatives and programs have been created to support racial, gender, and civic justice. Ultimately, we're all about justice, care, and connection for everyone.

SELF-RESPECT IS IMPORTANT FOR EVERY PERSON. WHEN you look in the mirror, you have to value who you see. If you don't respect yourself, then you have to do the work and make changes. Throughout the years of activism, it really felt like I was becoming the man I wanted to be. I'm not a perfect person by any means, but I have learned and grown from my mistakes and continue to evolve. Today, I feel that I've become the person that a young Wilmer would have looked up to. I intensely value my family, a sentiment that's felt for my extended family, too, my Latino community, and I stand in solidarity with all marginalized people groups. I love this country for the opportunities it has given me, and I want all people everywhere to be able to live with respect, progress, and freedom. I believe that anything is possible in the United States, and the only things that are impossible are the things you've told yourself are so.

Here's a small example of how welcoming and respectful this country can be toward immigrants. My mother is very supportive of me, but she likes to keep a low profile. During my hiatus years, she had never seen me speak about my activism and had only a cursory idea of my volunteer efforts, mostly through Spanish news services.

One Mother's Day a few years back, I decided to treat my mother to a surprise trip. She knew when we were going to leave, but she didn't know where we were going or why. I instructed her to pack some nice clothes. We got into the car and drove to the airport. She looked at her ticket and said in Spanish, "Dallas? We're going to Dallas?"

"Just wait and see, Mama," I said. "You're really going to enjoy this trip."

My mom had never been to Dallas, so she didn't know what the city looked like. When we landed, it was dark, and I still didn't tell her where we were. We took a car to the hotel, and I helped her to her room. I told her what time I'd meet her in the morning and to be dressed up. Early the next day, I put on a suit and met her in her room.

"I have a little speaking engagement I have to stop at first," I said. "Then we'll go and do our thing."

We rolled through the city. She was looking out the window, a bewildered grin on her face, enjoying the adventure. I'd instructed our driver to take us in the back way so the building wasn't recognizable when we arrived at our destination. We parked and climbed out. As we were walking through a green, leafy area, my mom asked, "Isn't this Jackie's garden?" I just chuckled.

A tour guide met us. "Welcome to the White House," she said.

My mother gave me a playful punch in the shoulder. "Wilmer! We're at the White House?!"

I laughed. "It was actually Dulles International Airport that we flew into. In Virginia."

Other people were near the entrance. We were instructed to come inside to a private room, which was all part of the plan. With two other people we waited inside the room for a few moments, then the double doors opened. Two uniformed White House security officers entered and stood on either side of the doors . . .

And in walked Barack Obama and Joe Biden.

They greeted us like longtime friends. "Wilmer, so nice to see you again," President Obama said in his deep, authoritative voice, then he greeted my mother in Spanish and gave her a little hug. She was grinning from ear to ear. He wished her a happy Mother's Day, then he said directly to her, "You should be very proud of your son. He's doing a lot of great work for his country."

It was such a surreal moment. My mother smiled at the president, then looked at me with a puzzled shrug, like, *Who is my son? What kind of work does he do that the president of the United States knows his name? And who am I, that the president speaks to me in my own language?*

We took some pictures, then our time was up. We went back to our car, and I took my mom to a special Mother's Day brunch. Over the meal she was quiet, and so was I, like we were both doing some serious reflection. As we dined on ham-and-cheese frittatas and drank champagne, it dawned on me that it hadn't been that long ago when my family had come to this country in search of a better life. In the years that had passed, we'd seen some hard times. But we'd also been able to realize our dreams. I knew that a third of my heart still identified with my mother's Colombian roots. Another third identified with my father's Venezuelan roots. Yet the final third, which had grown to eclipse the other portions, was now my spirit and soul. That third was enmeshed with the United States. I embraced my roots, but I was so deeply proud to be an American. The better future that we were now living, that better life, that's what I wish for everybody who comes to the United States.

CHAPTER 9

The USO

At first, it seemed like any other Tuesday morning. I was twenty-one years old, and we were a couple of seasons into *That '70s Show*. My alarm went off, and I skipped my workout, hitting the Snooze button a few times before rolling out of bed, hopping in the shower, getting dressed, and grabbing breakfast in the kitchen. It was about 7:00 a.m. I was just about to head out the door and to the studio when my pager went off. (Yep, I actually had a pager back then.)

911.

The message came from one of my best friends who lived on the East Coast. "911" meant she wanted me to call her quickly.

"What's going on?" I said into the phone.

"Turn on the TV," she said. "Now!"

Her voice was trembling. Full of alarm. I'd never heard her like this before. I switched on the TV.

"Whoa," was all I could say.

It was September 11, 2001. Every channel carried the same images. The first and second towers of the World Trade Center had been hit by hijacked Boeing 767s, and the South Tower had just fallen. Toxic smoke filled the New York City skyline. Flight 77 had crashed into the western side of the Pentagon, the nerve center of America's armed forces. Flight 93 had crashed in a field near Shanksville, Pennsylvania. As I stood in my kitchen in Los Angeles watching America's East Coast under attack on live TV, the North Tower collapsed in real time, right in front of my eyes. Suddenly, both of New York's tallest buildings had been reduced to rubble. Thousands of people were dying. Debris and charred paper rained from the sky. It seemed impossible that America could be hit by terrorists like this on our own soil. But it was happening. And it was very real.

My phone rang. It was a studio rep calling to say all rehearsals were canceled for the day. Everybody needed time to grieve and process the horror. All the rest of that day, I sat glued to my TV. I felt vulnerable. Uncertain. Angry. Fearful. Protective. Newscasters were speculating that more cities in America were going to be hit. Stadiums. Convention centers. Malls. Anywhere that people gathered in big numbers. Nowhere felt safe.

The next morning I jumped in my car and drove to the set, if only to be around other shocked people. On the drive over, I saw American flags flying everywhere. They flew in front yards and from awnings on storefronts, on hastily set up flagpoles all over the city, from the antennas of cars. All of America was grieving, and we were all grieving together.

On set, nothing felt the same. Ashton had a faraway look in his eyes. Mila was in tears. We all just sort of looked at each other and shook our heads. We tried to rehearse, to get on with our business, but nobody could find the punch lines that day. None of the scenes carried any rhythm.

A few days later, President George W. Bush toured Ground Zero, the smoking mass of rubble that used to be the Trade Center. He stood shoulder to shoulder with firefighters, police officers, and rescue workers. They were still searching for victims in the wreckage. He called to the crowd that had gathered around him, using a bullhorn to project his voice. Together, the city, the nation, and the world were mourning the loss of nearly three thousand people who'd died in the attacks. People of many more nationalities than just American had been killed. New York City is a melting pot for the world. Canadians. Australians. Argentinians. People from Bangladesh, Brazil, Chile, China, Colombia, France, Germany, India, Italy, Japan, Mexico, Philippines, South Korea, the United Kingdom, Venezuela, and many more countries. All had died at the hands of terrorists. The 9/11 event wasn't merely an attack on the United States. It was an attack on the world.

"I want you all to know," the president called out, "that America today—that America today is on bended knee in prayer for the people whose lives were lost here, for the workers who work here, for the families who mourn. This nation stands with the good people of New York City, and New Jersey and Connecticut, as we mourn the loss of thousands of our citizens."

In a moment that's now become famous in modern history, a lone rescue worker, straining to hear the president from the back of the crowd, shouted, "I can't hear you!"

The president called back, "I can hear you. I can hear you. The rest of the world hears you. And the people who knocked these buildings down will hear all of us soon."[1]

The crowd cheered, then soon picked up a chant. "USA! USA!"

I saw an energy born that day, an energy that was felt around the country and in the many other countries around the globe who love liberty and hate terrorism. We were all together. We were unified. The terror attacks needed to be answered.

DRIVING HOME FROM THE STUDIO A FEW DAYS AFTER the attacks, I tried to get my thoughts in order. Many people were enlisting, and although I wasn't afraid to fight for the right causes, I never wore the uniform. But I always wanted to serve. If I didn't become a soldier, what could I do? Was there some other way I could serve my country?

Those questions stayed with me for some time, although I didn't know where to land. A couple of years later, an answer began to emerge. I was walking through the Newark airport one evening when three young, uniformed soldiers came up to me and told me how much they loved *That '70s Show*. They were excited to meet me and bubbling over with words. Before I could get a word in edgewise, they thanked me for my role on the show.

They thanked *me*.

Instantly, I couldn't speak. I was too choked up. Here I was, so incredibly grateful for what they were doing. I should have been the one thanking them.

As we talked, they explained that they'd been deployed in the Middle East, and they'd felt a long way from home over there. They mentioned that our show was shown on the American Forces Network, a TV and radio broadcast service that gets sent to military personnel stationed overseas. We were being played at installations around the world. Guys on base would collect and trade *That '70s Show* DVDs like trading cards. Whenever they watched the show, it felt like they were home again.

I just had to sit with that information. The soldiers took some photos. I signed some autographs, shook hands, and we all gave each other hugs before saying our goodbyes. As I walked away, I was still shaking my head in disbelief. I reached my gate, and an idea began to form. It felt almost silly at first. But the more I thought about the exchange I'd just had, the idea didn't seem so silly after all. What if Fez showed up to say hello to the troops? He could tell some jokes, shake some hands. He might just encourage some people doing an extremely difficult job. He might bring some cheer to people who needed a small taste of home.

Ever since I'd been a kid growing up in Venezuela, I'd always had huge respect for Bob Hope. I used to watch him on TV all the time. He partnered with Frank Sinatra, Dean Martin, Marilyn Monroe, Jerry Lewis, Sammy Davis Jr., so many of the iconic performers of his day, and they traveled to military bases around the United States and overseas to entertain the troops with the United Service Organizations (USO). Together, they'd sing and perform sketches. Bob Hope had such a larger-than-life persona. His stage work appeared effortless for him. He was just having a good time with his friends and with all the people in the audience.

I knew the USO was like a booster club for the military. It's not run by the federal government. It's chartered by Congress, but it's a nonprofit organization that relies on the generosity of people, organizations, and businesses to support its activities. Whether a person is onstage with the USO, or serving meals, or handing out snacks, or helping troops transition from one location to another, or supporting the family members of the fallen and wounded, it's all run by volunteers.

I talked to my agents. They called the USO, and within a week a rep from the USO was offering me dates for a handshake tour, like a meet-and-greet with military personnel. That sounded good to me, but right away I wondered if I could do more. *Yo Momma* was just cranking up on MTV, and I thought, *Wouldn't it be cool if we brought the whole show over to entertain the troops?* I explained the show's premise to USO officials, and they were kinda like, "What the what?!" because it wasn't their usual fare. But I give the USO a lot of credit. They had no idea what they were getting into with *Yo Momma*, but they were still visionary enough to see that the show connected with the younger generation in a big way. They said yes.

We took *Yo Momma* over to the US troops in Germany first. I brought eight or nine performers and people who worked with the show, and Frankie J, the award-winning Latino singer. He'd been born in Tijuana and had come to the United States at age two, and he is deeply proud of his adoptive country. The auditorium was packed for the show. We warmed up the crowd with a DJ first and showed some video clips from the show. Frankie J came out and performed his hits "That Girl" and "Suga Suga" and a couple of other songs. Then our live *Yo Momma* contestants came out and took the stage. We'd set up an East Coast versus West Coast championship match, and they went to town on the jabs and roasts and jokes. Round one featured yo-momma one-liners. Round two showcased freestyle insults. Round three was all about delivering the perfect knockout joke, one joke to rule them all. It was an absolute riot.

Yo momma's so fat, the horse on her polo shirt is real.

Yo momma's so ugly, when she walks into a bank they turn off the cameras.

Yo momma's so dumb, she heard there was a serial killer on the loose so she went home and hid all the Cheerios.

The crowd stayed right with the performers, laughing and cheering and hollering their voices hoarse in all the right places. I took the mic near the end of the show and said a few simple but heartfelt phrases. "I just wanted to say on behalf of all of us here, not only onstage but back home, that we miss you, we appreciate you, and you make us proud to be Americans. Just know that we'll be waiting for you at home."

The show lasted for more than an hour, and when it was finished, we signed autographs, took pictures, and shook hands with the troops. I asked a few questions, but I did far more listening than talking. I heard story after story of why people joined the military. Most had joined because they'd felt a sense of duty, a calling. They wanted to make America and the world safe from terror. Some talked about how they'd become radar technicians or heavy-duty mechanics with the armed services; they were excited to learn a new trade and serve their country that way. Many talked about how the military gave them a sense of purpose and belonging. They were part of something larger than themselves. Everybody talked about how they valued freedom and opportunity. I felt my perspective expanding.

Later I heard that our first *Yo Momma* show with the troops almost didn't happen. Apparently, some of the higher brass were concerned about the contents of *Yo Momma*, that maybe it wasn't the right image for the US military. But once they saw our show, they could see that *Yo Momma* was all about having fun and certainly not about offending anybody for real. When I was onstage, I'd seen some high-ranking officers in the crowd. They were yukking it up along with everybody else. The show brought officers and enlisted personnel together.

During that same tour, we flew from Hohenfels to Stuttgart and performed for the troops a second night, then to Ramstein for a third show. Landstuhl Regional Medical Center was our next stop, where I expected to meet some of the wounded troops and move on. I wasn't prepared for major surgery on my own soul. When military personnel are wounded overseas, Landstuhl is the place where they're often flown first, where they get well enough to make the flight back to the United States.

For me, Landstuhl was my pivot. That's where my big internal shift occurred. Visiting troops in the hospital, I met many wounded soldiers, the men and women who have sacrificed so much. I saw firsthand their bravery and resilience. It was like this new depth of care showed up in my heart, a new capacity for compassion. It struck without warning, and it hit me hard. In Landstuhl, I realized I had a responsibility to say the right thing, to be thoughtful, careful, helpful, encouraging, no matter how traumatic a situation I was entering. My job during the shows was to entertain, to inspire, to help troops by bringing them a piece of home and setting their minds at ease. But at Landstuhl, my mission was to heal. Someone told me later that when you get hit hard with a strong sense of compassion like that, it's like God is working in your life. He's offering you a chance to make a difference in a difficult world. He's infusing you with a new sense of purpose.

A few months after my first trip, I returned to Landstuhl with Marine Corps General James Cartwright, vice chairman of the Joint Chiefs of Staff; model and singer Mayra Verónica; and my good friend comedian Russell Peters. It was November, just in time for American Thanksgiving, and before Landstuhl we held shows at Bagram Air Base in Afghanistan, Camp Liberty in Baghdad, and several other bases before visiting troops in Turkey and Greenland. Everywhere we went, we expressed our support and appreciation for the service members. It was a truly majestic trip, and it was the first time I'd been in an actual war zone.

Afghanistan and Iraq were red-hot, tense places. Everybody in my family was petrified for me before the trip, but I was excited. This was my contribution to the effort. On one leg of that trip, we were flying in an Osprey helicopter toward Fallujah. Flares shot out from the sides of the aircraft, and I wondered why. They were our flares. Once we landed, the colonel who flanked the general said, "Funny, no? We got locked on. Don't worry, they never hit anything." I had to think about that a moment. An Osprey will fire out flares to confuse incoming heat-seeking missiles. I guessed somebody down below didn't like us very much. Even then, I didn't feel scared. A lot of security surrounded General Cartwright at all times, and the armed forces did a beautiful job of keeping us safe and functioning on the tours. I wore a flak jacket everywhere and a helmet.

Then we returned to Landstuhl.

It had taken me some time before I could even try to put into words what I'd seen and felt at Landstuhl on my first trip. This second trip was similarly impactful.

In one room, a soldier was recovering from his wounds. When the nurse led us in, the soldier was waking up, but he hadn't opened his eyes yet. General Cartwright and I were the only ones from the tour in the room with him. Mayra and Russell were visiting other troops.

It felt solemn to be in that room with him. Like standing on sacred ground. The soldier was hooked up to all these tubes, and his face was turned to one side. General Cartwright stood on that side, and just then the soldier's eyes fluttered open and he started to focus his vision. It's extremely rare for troops in the field to see a four-star general. He looked at General Cartwright first, stiffened, and tried to raise his hand in a salute.

"At ease," the general said quickly, then talked to him in a low, kind voice. "You've made our country very proud, son. Your new mission is to go home and get better."

The general kept talking to him, murmuring bits of encouragement in reassuring tones, and after a couple of minutes, the soldier's posture sort of straightened out and he relaxed. He turned his head to see me. An extremely bewildered look came over his face.

His voice croaked. "*Fez?*"

We all chuckled, and I said, "Well, I'm sure you're more excited to see the general than me."

The soldier gave a little shrug and he spoke slowly. "Actually . . . I'm glad to see you too. But I have to admit, it still feels like I'm asleep. This feels like the most random moment of my life."

We didn't want to talk too long or tire him out. As we were getting ready to leave, he said to the general, "I just want to get back to my guys." I saw a slight wince pass over the general's face.

Later, after we were out of the room, I heard the news, and it conveyed to me anew how the ordinary people we refer to as military personnel are tasked with such difficult and extraordinary responsibilities.

The soldier's unit had been hit hard. He didn't know he might be the only survivor.

ONCE, ON A DIFFERENT USO TOUR, WE SLEPT OVER-night in one of Saddam Hussein's palaces. The Al-Faw, it was called. We were staying at Camp Liberty on Victory Base Complex near Baghdad. Surrounding the complex ran a line of blast walls and razor wire to guard against attacks from hostiles. Inside the complex, it was a different story. Hydro pumps and power plants were operating, and the water and electricity that Saddam had hoarded for himself for so many years was flowing freely to the Iraqi people again. The brutal dictator who had terrorized his nation and so many other parts of the world was dead and gone.

They say Saddam built a hundred palaces all for himself. The one I visited stood in the center of a man-made lake. Ducks floated on the surface. Fish leaped up from the depths and splashed in the sunlight. By early evening, a string of ground lights turned on and shined upward to illuminate the concrete palace walls, making the entire architectural crown jewel look like it was made of gold.

Inside the palace, our handlers let us wander from room to room in the 450,000-square-foot structure. The designs were ornate, the rooms enormous, the fixtures glittering. Apparently Saddam didn't come to Al-Faw much. But his sons, Uday and Qusay, liked to hang out there. Before his sons died in a gunfight in Mosul, they'd racked up a string of murder and rape offenses, and reports say they tortured Iraqi Olympic athletes and soccer team members who lost a match. Uday would have the athletes caned on the bottoms of their feet, shattering bones and permanently damaging tissue, so they could never run again. It's estimated that their father, Saddam, was responsible for the murders of at least half a million people. Saddam even ordered mustard and nerve gases to be used against his own citizens—men, women, and children—wiping out entire villages at a time. When I stared at that palace, it reminded me never to forget who the enemy was.

Later that evening, after dinner, I sat outside on one of the patios with two colonels, who flanked the general. A string of Black Hawk helicopters flew low over our heads, rattling our chairs, sending good shivers down my back. As the nighttime sky became calm again, we lit cigars and told stories about our childhoods, how we all longed for opportunity when we grew up. Tours such as this reminded me that all the effort was worth it.

After I toured the palace, I began to understand more of my own role in the war against terror. I wasn't a frontline soldier, but I often shared the same war zones. My role, if ever so small, was to help our defenders cope with the difficulties they were facing. If I could remind our people of the good things about home, maybe infuse a boost of strength, and never let them forget how much we appreciate their sacrifice, somehow that might push our military personnel to keep going on the days when it grew rough.

Understanding that vision helped me keep going myself. Over the years, I became addicted to serving with the USO. I kept going places. I kept doing shows. I entertained troops in Afghanistan, Iraq, Germany, Poland, South Korea, Djibouti, Greenland, Norway, Bahrain, Bavaria, on ships at sea, and at any number of domestic bases. I've done ten tours so far and counting. Within those tours, I've given more than fifty USO performances. I've hosted Backstage at the

USO, an entertainment event for service members and USO advocates, and I've supported USO galas back at home.

It feels like I'm just getting started.

Tours hold their share of challenges for a volunteer. Some nights, we slept only two hours, and the pace stayed grueling for days on end. We might shower twice during an entire trip. We'd do ten shows in five days and be traveling each night or during early morning hours to the next base. But even when the going got rough, I reminded myself it was far easier than what our military personnel were doing. I kept reminding myself of the why: *They are serving a larger cause, and I am serving them.* That's the gift. That's the exchange.

A FEW YEARS AGO WE FLEW TO VÆRNES AIR STATION in Norway, of all places, to bring a little bit of home to the marines and sailors deployed there in support of NATO and US European Command. The tour took place near Christmastime. In winter. I was freezing my ass off. I'm like, "What the hell are you guys doing over here?" And they're like, "We live here, dude. At least for now." Everybody was laughing and shaking hands, and our breath was coming out in huge vapor clouds in the frosty air. I stayed right in the moment, but man, normally I live in Southern California. I felt so cold!

Musician Kellie Pickler was on that trip, and we got to be great friends, and a few years later she became a USO Global Ambassador with me. We've done several other tours together now. Olympian Shaun White; comedian Jessimae Peluso; actor Milo Ventimiglia; DJ J.Dayz; five-time CrossFit champion Mat Fraser; and General Joseph Dunford, the chairman of the Joint Chiefs of Staff, were on that trip too. We all became close friends. In fact, on every USO tour I've taken, all the volunteers come back as friends. It's an incredible bonding experience, serving like that together.

While I was in Norway, I got to talking to some of the troops, and I asked if this was common, being away from their families during the holidays. They informed me that some 190,000 service members were on assignments away from home over that holiday season. They were serving ashore in such places as South Korea, Iraq, Germany, and Japan, and aboard ships in the Pacific and Atlantic Oceans, the Mediterranean Sea, and the Persian Gulf.

That made me feel incredibly grateful. Every year I celebrate the holidays with my family, and I don't think twice about it. But not everybody gets that experience. Year after year, I've celebrated birthdays and Fourth of July barbecues and Christmas and New Year's Eve all with my family, and there is no way I'd ever miss my mom's birthday. I'd been taking those moments for granted.

Plenty of military personnel are regularly away from their families on important occasions. The whole family sacrifices then. Maybe a father is deployed overseas, and he misses his daughter's ninth birthday. Or somebody's wife is serving on board a ship in the Atlantic, and she and her spouse can't celebrate their anniversary. When troops are gone like that, kids miss their parents; grandparents miss their adult-aged children. Everybody misses everybody. The more I talked to troops, the more I understood that being away from loved ones was one of their biggest personal challenges. Person after person said, "Yeah, it's really hard during the holidays."

So we tried to bring some cheer. Right there in Norway, we held a holiday feast with the troops. Everybody chowed down on turkey and roast beef, mashed potatoes and gravy, green beans, cookies, cakes, and pies, juice and eggnog. Wow, those guys could put away the eggnog. And then the poignant thank-yous started coming again. Not us saying thank-you to them. But them to us. I'd be sitting there eating, and a guy would come up to me. "Thanks so much for being here," he'd say. And I'd be like, "Are you kidding me? Thank *you* for being here!" That happened over and over during that meal. After being thanked about a dozen times, I felt so humbled. Who was I to gripe about the cold? Who was I to receive such gratitude?

On that same tour, we were scheduled to give ten performances in six days. We flew from Norway to Germany and Poland, then hopped to Bahrain, Iraq, Afghanistan, and the aircraft carrier USS *John C. Stennis* off the coast of the Persian Gulf. It was a lot of go, go, go, and everybody was exhausted by the time we returned home.

I'd done a few trips by then, and I remember coming home and looking at various memorabilia I'd gathered on these trips. In the military, they often give what they call "challenge coins" to people they respect. It's a special coin they get minted, not to use as currency but just to put in the palm of someone's hand as a gift. I've been given many coins, and I keep them right at my desk. On the back of one coin, Bob Hope's face is imprinted in the silver. I took a good long look at that coin, and I said, "Thanks, Bob. Thanks for all you did for the troops so that people like me could have that same experience today."

On another trip, I'd been given an American flag, one that had been flown over Ground Zero in New York City. It hangs in a frame on my office wall to this day. It's one of my most prized possessions.

THROUGH THE USO, I MET JANE HORTON. SHE GREW UP in Cleveland and went to college in New York, where she met a guy named Christopher. They dated, fell in love, and got married. Christopher trained as a sniper with the Oklahoma National Guard. He was assigned to the 1st Battalion, 279th Infantry Regiment, 45th Infantry Brigade Combat Team and was soon deployed to Afghanistan.

Yup, so what?
I love birds.

Marilyn and me. Mom used to go all out with the outfits. I had no say—hence my face.

Riding a horse at Disneyland, not knowing in just a few months I'd be riding a real one in Venezuela.

Graduating second grade. (Acarigua, Venezuela)

My first play.
(Acarigua,
Venezuela)

The reason why I still have an accent.
(Muholland Junior High, Van Nuys, mid 1990s)

My first English-language play. I have to admit I only understood half the words I was performing.

My Taft High School English class, in the mid 1990s. Definitely a C, maybe +.

Traveling the world with the three men I respect the most: Shaun White, Matt Fraser, and Milo Ventimiglia.

My brother, my mentor, and an icon of our community: Mr. Robert Rodriguez.

As soon as the rights closed at Disney, John Gertz surprised me with this epic gift.

Making one of our biggest memories and sharing it with our dear Tracy. (La Jolla, San Diego, California)

Just us, living our fairytale . . . also sweating my shirt off.

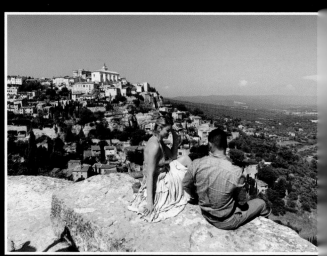

My little family.

(Photo credit: Giedre Gomes)

One of my guardian angels, Sir Marrok.

Showing my mother that Colombia can be more on screen.

Another milestone: recording Disney's *Encanto*.

(Photo credit: Jesse Grant/Getty Images Entertainment via Getty Images)

Cinco de Mayo at the White House with the fellas and my mom fourth-wheeling.

Everyone said
it was impossible,
but I got Mark Harmon
on Instagram.

*NCIS*verse.

USO tour
throwback.

The USO arranged a Blue Angels tour for my birthday.

Maj Nathan Miller   Lt Dan McShane

Blue Angels

USO duties. Baby,
it's cold outside.

New whip,
who dis?

What an honor for an entertainer to get to say thank you to the individuals who make this country one of the best in the world.

I carry the voices and the hearts of so many in my culture. With every stand comes a closer look at our brighter future.

(Photo credit: Kris Connor/
Getty Images Entertainment
via Getty Images)

Two months after arriving in country, on September 9, 2011, he was caught in an ambush in a remote eastern section of the country. Christopher didn't make it out alive. He was twenty-six years old. Killed in that same fight were Sergeant Bret Isenhower, also twenty-six, from Oklahoma, and Private First Class Tony Potter, only twenty. Tony's wife was pregnant with the couple's first child.

Grieving, Jane rolled up her sleeves and went to work. She wrote a bill to create congressional fellowships for what the military calls Gold Star families—people who've lost a family member while in the armed services. The widows and widowers. The parents and grandparents. The children.

She advocated for better health care and trauma services for military personnel. She sat on boards and served as a policy consultant to many groups that supported the troops. She worked to get scholarships so surviving spouses who needed more lucrative jobs could go to college. She flew to Afghanistan six times to continue her husband's legacy any way she could, representing the families of the fallen during her visits. She wanted to see the country where Christopher gave his last breath. Sometimes she helped out at Afghan orphanages. She met with Afghan leaders, and she's had top-level Afghan officials thank her for her husband's sacrifice. She launched a fund to help Afghan refugees, and she helped a female Afghan refugee relocate to the United States. Recently, Jane served as a senior adviser in the Office of the Secretary of Defense in the Pentagon.

Jane says that sometimes people ask her if it's all been worth it. Not just the work she does today but her husband's death. Her response startled me at first, until I started thinking about it in bigger ways.

"My husband wasn't mine," she said. "When I sent him off to war, I sent him off as America's. He belonged to all of us. So that question is really the question all of us need to ask. We all have to grapple with the difficulties that are presented by his death." Here, she looked straight at me and added, "I invite all Americans who value freedom to ask themselves, 'Was it worth it?'"

I sensed what she was hinting at. Freedom is never free. The fact that we can live where we want to live, start businesses, assemble together, vote, worship how we choose or not at all—these freedoms come with a steep cost. Her question changes how we see things; it prompts us to switch our perspectives from feeling entitled to feeling grateful. Christopher Horton was killed, but the rest of us are here. We are not broken. We are still strong. That dauntless spirit people such as Jane demonstrates is unbreakable. Like her, we can do something purposeful with that sacrifice that's been given for us. Christopher Horton gave so much so that we could live lives of purpose.

I WAS ON A BASE IN AFGHANISTAN, FOUR O'CLOCK IN the morning, and I couldn't sleep. I don't remember which tour this was, but it was back near the start. Dates and years and bases blur in my memory. We had to get our bags packed early so we could haul them to the C-130 and fly to our next show. My internal schedule was all mixed up from jetlag and the time difference. But the sleeplessness I was feeling that early morning was something different. I'd had about three hours of rest on my bunk with my eyes closed, and our wakeup call wasn't until 5:30 a.m., but I didn't want to go back to bed. I wanted to stay awake.

Quietly, I dressed, laced up my boots, and gently clumped out of the metal-framed Quonset hut where we were staying. Nothing outdoors was in motion yet. The desert smelled dry and fresh, and it seemed like the entire world was hushed except for the faint hum of the base's generators far across the compound. I took a deep breath of cold, crisp air and looked up. There's very little light pollution in the desert. Above me, the sky was sprinkled with a trillion gleams of starlight. For a long while I stood, humbled and awed, marveling at the celestial glow. I knew the sun would be up soon, and I'd be onstage again. I would shake hundreds of hands and listen to hundreds of beautiful stories, and I would need to continue to reach deep and give everything inside me. Already I was thinking about a new joke to tell when I first took the microphone. But this single moment was so quiet, so energizing, so peaceful. I just wanted to stay like this, at least for a while.

"Wilmer," I whispered to myself. "How crazy is this? You used to watch *RoboCop* over and over at that tiny theater in Venezuela. Now you're in Afghanistan with generals and colonels and celebrities, entertaining US troops."

I kept looking up. I kept searching the heavens.

You know sometimes how people say they actually hear the voice of God? I don't know if I can attribute what was happening in my heart that early morning to the voice of God, but I'm certain that God's presence could be felt in Afghanistan just like he is felt everywhere. It was like God was right next to me, there in the desert under the vast sky.

This voice said, *Wilmer, remember this: when a person has been given much, then much is required of him. You, Wilmer, have been given a lot. Sure, you've worked hard, but doors have opened for you in ways that aren't coincidences. You're here for a reason. The world is full of dark stories, and you've heard and witnessed some of those stories while on these tours. But your purpose is to keep spreading hope and light. And do more of it. Don't slow down. In fact, dig deeper and give a little more. All around you are selfless human beings. You're being inspired by them, and now you have a responsibility to inspire others. Keep going. Get up earlier. Stay up later. Do more with your life.*

When I came home from that tour, I was fired up. I'd seen that life could be bigger. I'd seen what it took for men and women to be on the front lines, and when I was honest with myself, I knew I wasn't doing enough. And my time for not doing enough was over.

I got back to work at the studio, and into the pace of meetings, calls, dinners, studying lines, time on set. But a change had come over me. A lot of growth can emerge from discomfort. I used to roll out of bed and head to the set, getting into work right on time. But after that tour, I started to wake up at four thirty each morning. I wanted to remind myself of that early morning in the Afghan desert. I wanted to seize each day.

I remember the first morning I did this back in the United States. I got up early and walked to my home gym, in a different building on my property than the main house. On the walk over, I looked up into the sky. The moon was out. The air was crisp. The morning felt energizing. My personal internal battery was getting recharged. After my workout was finished, I showered and dressed and still had forty-five minutes before I had to leave for the studio. So I decided to go in early and take care of a bit of extra work. After I got to the set and finished my extra work, I noticed that people were rolling in at the regular time, looking a little tired, searching for breakfast from the caterers. But already I was on fire. I'd been up for two hours before everybody else, and I knew that even then, I didn't have enough time to finish everything I wanted to accomplish that day.

Those early mornings have stayed with me. I've woken up at 4:30 a.m. ever since. The early mornings help give me the hours to achieve, execute tasks, and perform at a consistently high level. These days, in addition to being an actor and an activist, I run multiple production companies and take the lead on many projects. I do my best to amplify marginalized voices. And I try to facilitate the space that was never fully given to me in hopes that I can see other people achieve their dreams.

Serving with the USO and meeting hundreds upon hundreds

of troops has changed so much for me. I came to the United States as an immigrant with a dream, and over time I came to appreciate the American flag and understand that the American dream is real. Through my time with the USO, I've realized who is responsible for protecting the opportunity that I benefit from. I owe it to them, to this generation of military personnel, to ensure that what they're doing is respected, admired, and honored.

I never used to share much about my work with the USO in the media because it was so personal to me. I've come to understand that amplifying their stories is incredibly important. We need to never forget what they do. Amplifying and sharing their stories is one way we can honor the men and women who fight for the world's safety. I can say that touring with the USO has been one of the proudest accomplishments of my career.

In 2021, I became a USO Global Ambassador, helping others understand how important it is to support the military, encouraging Americans everywhere to follow our heroes' example in stepping up and serving. I am so grateful to the men and women of our military. They do much, so that we can do much with our lives.

CHAPTER 10

Tetris and *NCIS*

E arly one morning, a buddy came over to do a workout with me. He's an intense training partner, and we pushed the weights hard. Afterward, we alternated between a hot sauna and a cold immersion plunge, which can help with soreness and recovery. In between the two temperatures, he asked me about deals that didn't happen, the projects I've turned down and why. We talked about how success for an actor seldom comes from appearing in only one role. An actor builds a career in pieces, carefully choosing roles over years, even decades, hopefully a lifetime. Saying yes to the right opportunities is important. Then again, saying no to the wrong opportunities, or saying no to the right opportunities that come at the wrong time, is equally vital to success.

Back in 2007, I signed a first-look deal with FremantleMedia. They had produced *American Idol* and *The Price Is Right*, among other megahit shows. A first-look deal is when you create or identify potential TV shows, then help develop and deliver them. My production partner at the time, Danny Villa, and I set up offices at Fremantle's corporate headquarters in Burbank. We dug deep and worked on our best ideas.

Months rolled by. They looked at a bunch of stuff we had, and we looked at some stuff they had. A few ideas began to take shape, and a few were acquired by networks. But soon it became time to move on.

Within two years, my first-look deal went to another media company. I'd produced and hosted *Yo Momma* by then, and I'd been instrumental in shaping and starring in *Handy Manny* for Disney, so a lot of good buzz crackled in the room. An idea sprang up to do a show about a salsa school in Miami. Dance instructors would get involved in the lives of the adults taking their class, almost like therapists or life coaches. Picture Debbie Allen's *Fame* being remade for modern TV and meeting salsa culture. The tone of this show was fun, heartfelt, and compelling. We'd dig into the characters' lives, and they'd be sweaty and cool and happy in class, and after class they'd go to dinner and wrestle with deep matters together.

Somewhere in the process, an idea got thrown into the mix to create rivalries between characters. Part of the team wanted scandals, rage, and lots of casual sex. The idea didn't seem right to me anymore. Nothing against the company—our working relationships are still intact today, and lots of shows are infused with similar tensions, so the concept made sense on paper. But it seemed to me like a piece of integrity was lost. I needed to stick to my guns, be true to my instincts. So we didn't move forward with the show.

In 2010, my agents heard that the producers of *NCIS: Los Angeles* wanted to bring in a new cast member. The producers inquired about me. The existing cast members were all terrific actors and great people—Chris O'Donnell, Daniela Ruah, LL Cool J, and my friend Eric Christian Olsen—and the show itself was a spin-off of *NCIS*, the mother ship that the franchise is built around. *NCIS: Los Angeles* is a solid military drama and police procedural, still going strong today, more than a dozen years later. But I wasn't sure about saying yes. I was in the midst of my hiatus years, and I hesitated to commit to a prime-time series again. I was still exploring projects as a producer with my first-look deals.

My business manager called and strongly encouraged me to take a meeting with the producers. He thought it would be a perfect fit for me and my values, not to mention a lucrative job. NCIS stands for Naval Criminal Investigative Service. In real life, NCIS agents investigate criminal activities in the Navy and Marine Corps. The agents are well respected and highly skilled, and the show sought to honor their work. Procedurals such as this can stay on the air for a long time, my manager added, and they also do well in syndication, yielding consistent cash flow for years.

I agreed: honoring the military was part of my overall mission, so that appealed to me strongly and made me seriously consider the opportunity. But I had determined not to take an acting job merely because it looked appealing or would make lots of money. I was more interested in staying the course, playing characters in TV shows and independent movies that I believed in strongly. They were more fulfilling than lucrative.

It was hard to say no. My agents talked to the producers and writers, and they outlined to me the premise of the new cast member. They wanted him to be a Latino character. He'd be humorous but a badass, kind of like Martin Riggs in *Lethal Weapon*. I was more intrigued after their explanation, and I took a couple of meetings, which went well. I respected them and the cast and what they were all doing. But I knew something still didn't feel right. I vacillated back and forth. Maybe the timing wasn't right. I couldn't quite put my finger on it.

As a spiritual person, I asked God about whether I should take this opportunity. I listened for a good long time. The tap on my shoulder felt real. It felt like God was telling me, *Stay true to your vision.* I called my agents and told them to thank the producers for this opportunity. But I was going to trust my intuition. I said no.

I have to hand it to my agents, how they dealt with this. They're savvy businesspeople and their hearts are generous. They're my guardian angels, truly bonded in friendship by the exchange of artistry. They responded, saying they wanted me to take only the roles I believed in fully. The right roles at the right time. They understood.

A couple of days passed. I stayed confident about my decision, but I admit I questioned myself. Did I really do the right thing? As an actor, I had just passed up a golden opportunity. Who was I to say no to *NCIS: Los Angeles*?

I swear, in those moments of self-doubt, I could almost hear this same whisper . . .

Stay true to your vision.

. . . and exactly one week after passing on *NCIS: Los Angeles*, I got the call about reading for Tom Hanks's *Larry Crowne*.

Tom's my hero. I had absolutely zero reservations about this project. I said yes immediately. As it so happened, appearing in *Larry Crowne* turned out to be a feast of joy. Not only was Tom an incredible mentor, but I also learned a ton of things from coproducer Gary Goetzman, a wise Hollywood producer who had previously been an actor in *Swing Shift*, *Married to the Mob*, *The Silence of the Lambs*, and *Philadelphia*. The entire cast was great, and Tom and Gary were so selfless and caring. I thought, *Okay then, this is what can happen when you bet on yourself. This is what it means to go with your heart.*

THE NEXT COUPLE OF YEARS PASSED QUICKLY. I KEPT appearing in roles I wanted. I loved the work, and more than once I thought, *If I had compromised and given in to what made sense on paper, I wouldn't have been able to do all these other things.* That path led me to many incredible actors, producers, writers, directors, and entertainment insiders. They furthered my education about the craft of storytelling and the different genres of the roles I got to play. The smorgasbord of characters I portrayed pushed me to become a more grounded actor. I learned to trust myself.

Particularly in the three years from 2014 to 2016 when I did *From Dusk till Dawn*, my career turned extremely busy again. Multiple offers started coming in. Any artist must put hours into fine-tuning the craftsmanship of their specific performing art, and it was an exciting time for me, despite my long hours. In my last season of *From Dusk till Dawn*, filmed in Austin, I also appeared in the TV series *Minority Report*, filmed in Vancouver, British Columbia, and *Grey's Anatomy*, filmed in Los Angeles. Coordinating the logistics of travel was zany. I'd shoot one show, speed to the airport, jump on a flight, take a short nap, then awake to study the next script. It went like that, from set to set and flight to flight, week after week. As if I weren't already busy enough, during that same time I also made a pilot for CBS Studios called *Four Stars*. (People called it beautiful and incredible, but there were too few slots available for the show to get picked up.) For a while, I actually helicoptered from sets to airports and back again so I could keep on schedule.

One evening I was on a flight between Los Angeles and Vancouver, and the guy in the seat next to me saw that I was reading a script and struck up a conversation.

"You're on TV?" he asked. "You think TV actors get any respect? I thought every actor only wants to be in the movies. They say that's where you hit the big time."

"Perhaps," I said. "But have you ever considered how audacious it is for an actor to be on TV?"

He shifted in his seat. "Audacious?"

"People see a movie once. Maybe twice. A film actor tells the story of a character and he's done. But on TV, audiences get to live and grow with a character. Every week. Month after month. For years on end. You have to tell hundreds of stories, and they all live on TV. A TV actor really needs to have the stamina to tell deep and relatable stories over a long stretch of time. A good TV actor must stay worthy of being watched."

"Huh." He scratched the back of his neck. "I've never thought about it like that. So, what's the big secret of staying successful on TV?"

I smiled. "You gotta really hate sleep."

IN EARLY 2016, IT ALL CAME FULL CIRCLE. I WAS FINISH-ing up my run on *From Dusk till Dawn*, wondering what I might do next, when the phone rang. Six years after the original phone call, *NCIS* called again. This time it was the mother ship asking if I wanted to be a regular on the show. It wasn't one of the franchises. It was *NCIS*, the original flagship.

As strange as it might sound, I still hesitated. It wasn't because I didn't respect the show. In fact, it was the opposite. The show was such a solid hit, doing so incredibly well. *NCIS* was voted "America's favorite television show" in 2011, and during 2012–2013, it was the most-watched TV series in the United States. At the start of 2016, when *NCIS* called me for the second time, the show had been running for an astonishing thirteen seasons already and was still the number one flagship show of CBS Studios. In 2016, nearly thirteen million viewers were tuning in to watch *NCIS* every week, at a time when nearly every other show on TV was fighting to bring in four to five million viewers. Mark Harmon, starring as Special Agent Leroy Jethro Gibbs, was the man.

My first thought was, *Wow! How cool. But I don't think the show needs me.* One of my agents, another of my guardian angels, Nancy

Mendelson Gates, encouraged me to go ahead and just take the meeting. This time, it was the head of CBS Studios, the president of CBS Studios, David Staff, and the CBS executive assigned to *NCIS,* Amy Rosenbach (today the president of CBS Network), who wanted me on the show. "They're being kind to request you," Nancy added. "*NCIS* is the best job in Hollywood these days. That's an opportunity that doesn't come along every day."

So I took the meeting with Gary Glasberg, the showrunner at the time (sadly, he would pass away a few months later, in September 2016, at age fifty). He met me in a small coffee shop in West Hollywood. He was a straight shooter who'd seen the pilot I'd done for CBS, the one that hadn't been picked up, and he'd liked my performance a lot. "*NCIS* is up for a change," he explained, saying that Michael Weatherly, who played Senior Field Agent Anthony DiNozzo, was leaving. But no, they weren't seeking to replace him. They wanted to create a new character with a different tone.

"To be honest, we need to infuse new elements into the show," Gary said. "*NCIS* has performed to a great level for all these seasons, but to survive, the show needs to innovate."

By this point, one of the few consistent actors of color they'd had on *NCIS* was Cote de Pablo, a Chilean American actress. Even though she is Latina in real life, she'd played a character named Ziva David, portrayed as an Israeli Mossad officer turned *NCIS* agent. Cote had left the show at the start of season eleven. Another actor, Duane Henry, played the smaller role of former British MI6 officer Clayton Reeves. Duane, who is Black, appeared on two seasons of *NCIS* before being killed off. Rocky Carroll, also Black, joined the cast in episode three as a supporting character but wasn't a lead. I understood what Gary was hinting at. CBS was going through a transformative period.

"We'd like to build a new character from the ground up," Gary added. "One you're excited to play. We have ideas, and we want your input. We're very open to the collaboration."

I liked what I heard, but I had one more important question. "Thirteen seasons is an incredible run already. Are people just phoning it in? Or is everybody still excited to be there?"

Gary grinned. "Come to the set. You're gonna like what you see."

On the drive back to my office, I thought about my activist work and all the larger conversations I was championing about how we needed to see more Latinos in the mainstream. My character wouldn't be a Latino bad guy. He'd be a good guy. Wherever I looked, I saw vacancy signs in the industry, and the time was right: I wanted in. I called my agent. "I love the vision Gary just cast for me. What's the next step?"

"Talk with Mark Harmon," she said. "You won't need to do a chemistry read, because they already love you, and they're inches away from making you an offer. Still, you'll need to talk with Mark. He's got a lot of say in how the show runs."

Mark was already a legend. Everything he did turned to gold. Back in college at UCLA, he'd been the Bruins' starting quarterback for two years. He'd graduated with honors and pursued a degree in communications. After appearing in a number of smaller roles, he'd played Fielding Carlyle on the smash hit *Flamingo Road*, then landed a lead role in the critically acclaimed *St. Elsewhere*, followed by another lead role on the hit *Chicago Hope*. He'd been nominated twice for a Primetime Emmy and won a zillion other awards. Once, Mark saved a teenage boy from a burning car. I mean, the guy was a hero both on and off the screen.

We touched base by phone. He'd also seen the pilot I did for CBS, and he liked my performance. "We'd be happy to have you here," Mark said. "But two things are important. First, it only works if you want to be here."

"I'd love to work with you, Mark," I said. "I'm very respectful of the work you've done."

"Second, things work a little different on set," he added. "People really like this job. They've been with us for a long time." He paused, then outlined some of his expectations for the show. I sensed the call was just a process that gave Mark peace of mind. I came away feeling that I didn't want to let him down.

My agent was right. After my conversation with Mark, an offer came. I signed on initially for two years. I started appearing regularly in the show in fall 2016 at the start of season fourteen.

Nobody knew for sure if I would jell with the cast. Any show can bring in a promising actor only to have a new character fall flat with fans. Just like when I'd built Fez, I promised myself I would swing for the fences. I'd determined to make bold moves and bring clear and unique opinions about who my characters would be. I wondered if I could do this with my new character, Special Agent Nick Torres.

From the moment I showed up on set, I sensed an immediate harmony. The show already knew itself. The writers and actors understood how to be efficient. The *NCIS* actors came in, took their marks, and delivered their lines. They were all friends afterward. I'd been on sets before where it seemed like nobody could find their footing. Sometimes we'd stay on set until midnight, reworking scenes over and over. But on *NCIS*, nobody messed up. Everybody went home by 6:00 p.m. Not because they were exhausted but because they'd come in prepared and the job was done. Their energy was professional and confident.

I was joining a dream team.

THE PRODUCERS INVITED ME TO HELP DESIGN MY character, but one of the first ideas I brought to the table proved disruptive. I didn't necessarily set out to cause trouble, but nobody liked my idea at the start. I stuck with it. I chose to have Nick not wear the iconic *NCIS* jacket on camera. Every other special agent wears the jacket. It's a part of the uniform, a badge of respect. But Nick Torres decided he wasn't going to put it on.

My action was met with hesitation at the studio at first, because they assumed the fans would want to see me wearing the jacket. But I wanted everybody to sit with this tension for a while, before I—and my character—explained the reasons.

Nick starts out as a lone wolf, a man used to solving problems with the law and his brawn. He doesn't work well with others, and he doesn't understand the value of depending on other people or trusting others for his safety. Born in Panama, Nick grows up close to everybody in his family except his father, who's abandoned the family and is presumed dead. Years later, Nick finds out the truth. His dad is actually alive. He'd left the family to go undercover with the CIA. But that doesn't change the fact that Nick grew up having to teach himself how to be a man. And it doesn't help them reconcile either, particularly when Nick's father abandons him again as an adult.

When Nick first joins the NCIS team, he's no stranger to law enforcement. He'd been an NCIS deep-cover agent for years. Nick had gone missing for six months, and his sister searched for him, blowing Nick's cover and endangering his family. Gibbs, played by Mark, brings Nick onto the NCIS team to help solve the case and keep his family safe. Gradually, Nick buys into the values of working together. He's cool at the start, but he's also cautious. Slowly through the seasons, we worked to have Nick accept that a team cares for him. We started giving him higher personal stakes. He works well with Special Agent Tim McGee, played by Sean Murray; with Special Agent Ellie Bishop, played by Emily Wickersham; and with Gibbs. Eventually, he becomes the protector of the team. He learns how to confide in his colleagues instead of punching first and explaining later.

So why wouldn't Nick wear the jacket?

Because at the start, I didn't believe Nick had earned the right to wear it. He was coming in as an experienced outsider, and he could work effectively on his own, but he was still an outsider, and he couldn't just roll in and immediately be one of the team. He needed to show everybody, including himself, he had what it takes. He wasn't disrespecting his team by not wearing the jacket. It was the opposite. A sign of respect.

When Nick finally puts on the jacket near the end of season two, and all this is explained, it's a moment of release. Nick is finally joining the team for good. He's earned the jacket. He's proud of his work, and everybody on the team is genuinely proud of him. The superfans went wild. They were like, "Finally!"

When we look back now, years later, everybody agrees this was a smart move. It helped my character develop a more personal journey. He grew, learned, hurt, and healed. I give the showrunner, writers, and producers a lot of credit for supporting this decision. Even though they didn't understand my choice about the jacket at the start, they stuck with me, wrote strong storylines for my character, and let Nick have room to run.

ALTHOUGH I'D CAUSED SOME TENSION, I'D STILL wanted to come in as an immediate team player. I wanted to be a joy to work with from the start.

Mark knew what he wanted. He was precise, and he delivered, time and time again. Mark jumped on board with me personally and with my character. We discovered we had a mutual love of classic cars, and we'd email pictures of cars back and forth. He'd tell me stories from his career, and I loved hearing them. He always listened. And he always made it clear he was there to support me. We soon became close friends.

The support showed up on-screen too. Nick experiences a string of letdowns over the years, and Gibbs ends up becoming a father figure to him. The rest of the team helps Nick cope. Gibbs never lets him down.

Right from the start, everybody expressed an openness to finding a different rhythm with my character. The cast met me halfway, and they welcomed the new ideas and differences I brought to the show. I wanted to make things super fun on set. Soon, I just started being myself, cracking jokes and telling stories. Everybody in the cast was so great, and they joined in the fun. Sean Murray was always supportive. He's a legacy character who'd been with the show from the start, and he worked hard to transfer his character into a senior leadership role as the seasons passed. I also loved working with David McCallum, who plays Dr. Donald Mallard, the team's (now-former) chief medical examiner; Brian Dietzen, who plays Dr. Jimmy Palmer; and Pauley Perrette, who played forensic scientist Abby Sciuto. Jennifer Esposito, who played Special Agent Alex Quinn the first season I was on the show, was terrific to work with. Emily Wickersham was always lovely to be around. She's incredibly talented and hardworking.

Apparently, for some time Mark had refused to have any pictures of him posted on social media. He insisted the photos were too unofficial. Our publicists thought it would be impossible to capture something candid about Mark and post it. I'm like, *What's the big deal? Mark's so nice.* I walked straight over to him and said, "Hey, Mark, can I take a picture of you to post?" He said, without missing a beat, "Yeah, sure, Will." They say I took the first-ever social media picture of Mark. I emailed it to the network, saying, "Was that so hard? You owe me three hundred dollars for this picture—and I'll take it all in pennies." Everybody had a good chuckle about that—then they delivered. It was hilarious! Have you ever seen three hundred dollars in pennies?! I guess the network had the last laugh when I had to carry it to my car.

Other than some questioning letters about me not wearing the jacket, the bulk of fan mail we received from the start was highly affirming of Nick Torres. Truly, I wasn't expecting how well the audience would respond to this character and love his presence on the show so much. For that, I'm so grateful to all the fans. This was a return to prime time for me, and although I had appeared in lots of shows in the years since Fez, this new character was such a departure from my roots in comedy. A number of fans wrote to say that once they found out I'd been Fez, they couldn't believe I was the same person. I took this as a compliment. I wanted Nick to be radically different than Fez. I was returning to the prime-time viewers who'd known me from the start, but now I was taking them on a new journey.

Early on, I indicated to the writers and producers on *NCIS* that I wanted to prove myself, and I was fine with tackling the most difficult scenes they could give me. Specifically, I asked if Nick could do more action scenes. I didn't want him to get into bar fights. I wanted him to do more dangerous stuff. So the writers began laying that out for me. Gradually, the fights and explosions and stunts became more elaborate. I performed many of my own stunts, but when they became too elaborate, I'd depend on stuntmen. Along the way, with me staying in my stunt scenes for as long as possible, on many occasions I'd get bruised up, blow out a hamstring, throw out a shoulder, or get punched in the face. All of that happened for real. My mother watched the show with me every week. One day she sat me down and took me to task. I had responsibilities, she said, so I needed to start taking better care of myself. I was being too much of a knucklehead, saying, "Put me in, Coach, put me in!"

I listened to her advice. These days, I have great collaboration with my stunt doubles. I still do a lot of stunts myself, but they will often take falls on motorcycles for me, get run over by cars, and do parkour stuff, running up and down the sides of walls. Even so, it can get dangerous for me. I'm still going to be Wilmer. One time a garage blew up with me nearby, and I definitely smelled my arm hair burning. I've done martial arts for years, and I've studied kickboxing and MMA fighting, so I feel confident on set when it comes to a fight. Even so, I can't tell you how many times I've been punched for real during the middle of a fight scene. It goes both ways. I've punched lots of stuntmen by mistake too. In the movies, an actor might rehearse for three months, then shoot the scenes. On TV, an actor rehearses for an hour, sometimes less, and then shoots. There's not enough time to choreograph every move.

One of my favorite episodes of *NCIS* is when Nick needs to go undercover into a cage-fighting ring to solve a murder. Canadian actor Zane Holtz guest-starred in the episode, and his character and my character clashed a lot. The fans loved it. He and I had both been on *From Dawn till Dusk*, and we're terrific friends in real life. I'm the godfather of his daughter.

In that storyline, the initial plan is to have the undercover Nick fight another undercover agent, so there would be no great danger involved. But at the last minute, Nick is forced to fight someone else, a huge, well-muscled, tattooed beast of a man. While other agents are monitoring the fight and working furiously to solve the crime, the fight begins. Nick punches and kicks and does his best, but he takes a beating from his larger opponent. When I'm getting slammed to the ground, that's me in the scene, and that hurts for real. I stopped plenty of punches for real too. When I was on the ground, the guy was pounding me for real, and that totally hurt. My stunt double jumped in for several shots, but for most of those scenes, it was me. I have friends who are MMA fighters in real life, and they watched the show and said it all looked accurate. That felt good. I wanted to honor the MMA community with that episode.

The episode works on a deeper level too. Even though he's so bloody and bruised, Nick refuses to tap out. He's taken a lot of hits in his life, and now it's almost like he's got a death wish. He refuses to quit. When it looks like all hope is gone, he rises up off the mat and keeps fighting, finally beating the bigger man's ass.

Later, Nick explains to Dr. Jimmy why he wouldn't give up. Too many people have abandoned him. Nick wanted to shut out everybody to avoid being hurt again. He'd given up hope. But he came to his senses, whether from pain or due to determination, and decided to keep fighting. Jimmy's wife had died recently in the show, and he told Nick that he felt the same way. Together, they decide that if they're ever going to heal, they need to help each other walk a better road. It's a powerful episode, one that shows the benefit of developing close friendships.

AT THE CONCLUSION OF SEASON TWENTY, I HAD appeared in more than 150 episodes of *NCIS*, and I'm now well on my way to hitting the magic two-hundred mark, the same number I did for *That '70s Show*. It's amazing that *NCIS* has been on so long. Twenty years now and counting. New episodes are still being produced, and *NCIS* is syndicated all over the world in a bunch of different languages. We've added many new characters since I joined, incredible actors all. Mark left the show in season nineteen, and we miss his presence, but *NCIS* shows no signs of slowing down. To date, *NCIS* is the third-longest-running scripted, non-animated prime-time series in the United States, bested only by *Law and Order* and *Law and*

Order: Special Victims Unit. It's amazing to think that since the show's inception in 2003, babies have been born and grown up and gone to college. Their parents watched the show when it was first on, and now the kids are watching it too.

Sometimes I wonder what would have happened if I'd just stayed in the same lane my whole career up to this point. I could have chosen that route. After I'd played Fez, I could have stuck to comedy, recreating the same zany character. But as much as I appreciate Fez and the start he gave me, I needed room to move. I've chosen to stay true to my larger vision and play many different roles. I'm often still recognized as Fez, but I haven't been typecast. That's a win.

I feel so incredibly honored to be a part of *NCIS*. Being on the show has given my family and me a beautiful stability. It's let us stay in Los Angeles and not need to move around the country or the world on various shoots. Nick Torres has become a real contributor to *NCIS*. He's been welcomed by the fans, and I can't wait to see what we do with Nick next.

The other day, I started thinking about the roundabout way I came to *NCIS*. It was during a rare spare moment for me, and I was lounging in my family room with a beer, playing a game of *Tetris*. It's that classic video game where different-shaped tiles descend toward the bottom of the screen. The goal is to join all the tiles together to make one continuous grid. *Tetris* sounds easy until you play it, because the game is based around a big puzzle. Each tile comprises four linked cubes, yet the tiles come toward you in different arrangements: four cubes in a straight line, vertically or horizontally; an L shape; a Z shape; a perfect block; a stacked line of three with one cube sticking out in the middle. As I played, I rotated each shape as it descended and moved it around to see where it would best fit.

This idea dawned on me that my life has been a lot like a game of *Tetris*. I haven't been sure where every piece will fit, particularly at the start of any new era. Various pieces have come at me and prompted questions about which way to turn. I've spun pieces around and moved them from side to side. When I first said no to *NCIS: Los Angeles* in 2010 because the timing wasn't right, I had no idea that I'd get another call to be on the main *NCIS* show in 2016. In the meantime, spinning pieces of my life saw me portraying a wide swath of characters and growing as an actor in an era that proved rich and fertile.

In the end, everything connected. Some call this destiny. I call this faith. A recognition of a guiding hand. As I finished my game of *Tetris* and put it away for the night, I thought, *Everything truly aligns.* When you welcome mystery, all things can work together for good.

CHAPTER 11

Holding the Same Pen

Marrok loves to snooze on the rug when I'm working in my home office. Many evenings, I take him for a walk in our neighborhood. He's a lovable but fierce Belgian Malinois, a few years old now. Sir Marrok was one of King Arthur's honorable knights in the battle against Lucius, the emperor of Rome. I chose my dog's name carefully. He's strong, tall, powerfully built, and loyal, honorable in every way. He could go to battle if he had to, defending those he loves. But he's not battle oriented in spirit. The snooze is more his style. If he's up for an adventure, we go outdoors and play in the park. For a long season, when it was just me at home, I'd put in full days of work, then return to a lonely house. Marrok was indispensable then. He and I would watch movies and hang out, just a man and his dog. But things have changed.

When Marrok and I are out walking, the evening shadows fall, and I think about my own family. My love, Amanda. We share our days and nights together and keep looking forward to the future. Our three-year-old daughter, Nakano, is delightful in every way. She has dimples like her mother and jokes like her daddy. In a few moments when Marrok and I return home, I'll kiss Amanda, and we'll spend the rest of the evening catching each other up on our days and being close. When it's time for our daughter to be put to bed for the night, we'll carry her to her bedroom, sing her a song, read her a book, whisper a prayer in her ear, and tell her we love her to the moon and back. "*Te amo*, chookie."

Any story about the family I have today springs from what I learned from my family of origin. Marrok knows my parents well, too, and he'll often sit beside either of them in pure loyalty. They are his heroes, and they are my heroes, too, my mother and father. We are all close today.

Now that I am an adult with a family of my own, I understand more fully the depth of sacrifice and love that parents go through for their children. These days, I never underestimate what my parents taught me about the importance of family. So much of what I learned about love, about the truer aspects of selflessness and giving to another person, I learned from them. They modeled a loving marital partnership for me. My mom and dad did everything they could for our family, often sacrificing their own needs and wants to make sure that we children had a better life, a quality education, and more resources than they did. They wanted us to dream bigger than they were able to do—and then fulfill those dreams. They laid down their own lives for us so that we could soar.

My sisters and I experienced an incredibly loving home growing up. For many years we didn't have much money, but a shelter of support and care was always present. There was never a moment where my parents embittered me or suppressed my dreams. On the contrary, if I wanted to take acting lessons or play soccer, they did whatever they could to help me achieve my goals. If I wanted to audition for commercials, my dad would scrape together his loose change for gas money to drive me to the studio.

Each parent infused in me a different set of values. My mother taught me loyalty, to be responsible, disciplined, and accountable. My father taught me generosity, to celebrate, and how to be a host. My parents never saw anyone as a stranger. Mom and Dad welcomed everybody into their home, and those guests would leave in time with a kind word and a full stomach and maybe even be a little tipsy from a few good glasses of wine. Together, my parents modeled a heritage of hospitality and values. They are both patient people who give much and honor those around them.

My parents would be the first to tell me that a successful marriage is about a committed collaboration. And they had a successful marriage for many years. But nothing came easy. The strain of selling everything in Venezuela, coming to America with three young children, struggling with low-paying jobs in a culture where a different language was spoken, and ensuring that each of their children was fed and clothed and doing well in school and had medical care—that all took its toll on my parents.

My father treated my mother like a queen in the limited time he had with her each day. He worked long hours, and when he came home, he was tired. Even so, regularly he gave her flowers and took her and the family out for dinners. He brought a sense of celebration into the house, and he invited each family member into the celebration he created. My mother ensured my father had everything he needed. She was tired at the end of each day too. But his clothes were always crisply ironed. Each evening she prepared a delicious dinner for the family. She cared so much for him. They created special times for us as children and celebrated all the holidays with us, working to instill in us a sense of tradition and heritage.

I integrated these values. I saw how things need to be. I look back on the good times in our family and I cherish them. I look back on the hard times and appreciate the sacrifices they made. Those sacrifices translate into the man I eventually became and into the world I inherited.

The fact that my parents' relationship didn't last makes me appreciate their sacrifices even more.

Coming to America for them was a high-stakes gamble that demanded from them a new level of hard work and stress. It was nothing short of trauma. They were torn from their friendships and support system back in Venezuela, and for several years they fought for our survival, just to make sure we had a roof over our heads. They bonded as marriage partners through those difficulties, but they also suffered. Eventually, and sadly, the stress of their new lives turned their marriage relationship into a coparenting relationship only. When we kids were at last gone and out of the house, my mother and father looked at each other and said, "What now?"

To this day, they have not divorced. They are still married, and they both live on my property, but they live in different houses, and they don't consider themselves a couple. I was twenty-four when they made this decision. As unfortunate as this arrangement may sound, I believe they do better these days when there's a bit of space between them. They are free to live their own lives. They still interact with each other regularly, and there's a mutual respect. They love spending time with all their children, and they immensely enjoy being grandparents. I sometimes wonder if we were all still living in Venezuela, whether they'd still be happily together in love. That question can never be answered definitively, but even the question makes me appreciate their sacrifices more fully. In coming to their new country, they sacrificed everything. Eventually, even their marriage.

WHEN I REACHED MY LATE THIRTIES, I CAME TO A crossroads personally. I'd always imagined getting married and having a family of my own. By then, everything seemed to be coming together so well in my career. I was an artist and an entrepreneur, a man devoted to his people and his Latino heritage and his new country of the United States. I loved my work on *NCIS*, and it seemed like so many great blueprints and infrastructures had been developed and built around my life. But I knew that one important piece was still missing: I was all alone.

Family has always meant everything to me; I'd seen the good lessons modeled by my parents. To build and keep a successful marriage, each person needs to make the other person a priority. I knew marriage requires focus and work, and my schedule was always so full. But in my quietest moments, I knew I didn't want to stay single. My life was joyous, and I had lots of friends. Even though I could walk next door to the house I bought for my mother and visit with her anytime, or I could walk to the guest house on my property where my dad lives and hang out with him, or I could call up my sisters and my nephew, Christian, and we'd all have fun together . . . something was missing. I still wanted baby toys across the floor.

One morning after a workout, a revelation came to me. My mind is so clear during those times, and after each workout I feel energized and lucid. I was sitting in a salt bath to help with the post-workout soreness, reflecting on where my life had come, and I said to God, "I sincerely feel content to stay alone. I'm okay with devoting myself to my work, if that's everything you have for me. But if not, please make it very obvious."

I showered and dressed and drove to work. That day, like the pattern of many of my days, was filled with studying and phone calls and performing on set, putting everything I had into my artistry. I came home that night, checked in with my parents, phoned friends, and hung out with Marrok. The day was the same as the one before it, but it was almost like I could feel a new energy on the move. When you tell God you're ready for a new stage of life, God hears you loud and clear and says, *Okay, I'm going to make it obvious. Get ready for life to change.*

It was about two weeks after that prayer. A friend, someone I respect and trust a lot, talked to me about a woman she knew and showed me a picture of the woman named Amanda. In the photo, she had short blond hair and blue eyes and was wearing a cool jean jacket and looking steadily into the camera. Amanda was gorgeous, and a twinkle in her eye said she was smart and playful and fun too. But honestly I didn't think much about the exchange that day. I had forgotten my prayer.

A few days later, the same friend was like, "You guys want to connect?" And I was like, "Wait, who is this person again?" And she was like, "Amanda. You guys should meet."

I wasn't thinking romance at the start. But to be perfectly honest, I also knew that I couldn't get Amanda's picture out of my mind. There was just something about her. I felt like I needed to know this person.

So we connected. At first, we just exchanged a few messages, all friendly conversations, really casual. Amanda lived in Los Angeles but was all set to move to Miami in a couple of months so she could focus on her work as a certified scuba divemaster and model. She loves the ocean and the outdoors. We talked about Miami. I'd been there often, and we chatted about restaurants and beaches and the best places to eat sushi.

We agreed we should meet in person someday. There was zero agenda. She reminded me a few times that she was moving cross-country soon, and we were both aware of that. But sometimes, we both agreed, it's just fun to meet up with someone and have a good talk. You see if your values align. That's the best place to allow a friendship to begin.

On the day that worked best for both of us, I was heading out on a trip later in the afternoon, but my schedule gave me four hours to kill before I needed to be at the airport. Amanda and I met up in a coffee shop in LA and talked. And wow—four hours zipped by in a flash. We were both very open with each other, just sort of unpacking our thoughts in this honest, like-minded way. She likes sunsets and baseball and camping and traveling, and her soul is full of sunshine. After we said our goodbyes and I headed to the airport, I thought, *Even if she's moving to Miami soon, somehow I know we're going to stay friends.*

When I came back to Los Angeles, we met again. This time at a restaurant over dinner. I found out she's half Mexican and half white, and she'd grown up in a close-knit family where her dad spoke Spanish fluently. After her mother was diagnosed with stage 4 ovarian cancer, Amanda had shaved her head in solidarity and moved back home to take care of her. Sadly, her mother passed in 2014, but Amanda has stayed fiercely true to her mother's legacy and has run races and raised money in support of ovarian cancer awareness and finding a cure. Amanda told me she misses her mother every single day—her laugh, her smile, her incredible strength. Each year on the anniversary of her mom's death, Amanda goes to the ocean to commemorate this amazing person.

I could relate to that depth of love in a family. I'd do anything for my parents.

At that same dinner, I spent a lot of time studying Amanda's face, the message behind her eyes, and even though we had said we weren't looking for a relationship at the time, I wondered if maybe our friendship might develop further. I asked a few careful questions about the way she saw life and about what she wanted in the future, and she clarified a few important things. Namely, while she wasn't necessarily looking for a relationship, if a relationship happened, she wouldn't object. We held hands on our way to the car, and that was our turning point, the day we threw ourselves into the deep end. I looked up at God and silently said, *Wow.*

Not long afterward, Amanda and I went to a neighborhood theater with my longtime best friend, Tadao, and his wife, Nicole. They know me well, and they were instantly at ease with Amanda, and she with them. It was like she had always been a part of our group. Tadao and Nicole were caring for the young daughter of one of Tadao's friends. The girl had tagged along for dinner that evening and mentioned she was fascinated with the ocean. Amanda spent a lot of time answering the girl's questions, explaining scuba diving to her and chatting about the amazing world that can be seen underwater. Out of the corner of my eye, I just watched them talk. Amanda interacted with the girl so effortlessly. She listened so attentively. That's when I knew she'd be a great mother.

We were together all the time after that. We took day trips to San Diego with friends. We ate lunches and dinners together and went for evening walks with Marrok. Amanda's mother had loved Disneyland, so I took Amanda there on a date. A couple of good friends came with us, and as we walked through the park, a beautiful butterfly landed on Amanda's backpack. Amanda held out her hand, and the butterfly flew straight to her and held on to her finger. Carefully, she moved her hand close to her heart, and for some time we walked through the park like that, with the butterfly attached to Amanda. When it came time to go on her mother's favorite ride, Amanda released the butterfly onto some nearby leaves. After the ride was over, the butterfly was still there, so Amanda held out her hand, and the butterfly flew to her again.

"I think I'm going to cry," Amanda whispered. It had been six years since her mother last took her to Disneyland. Amanda saw the butterfly as a sign that her mother's presence remained close to her. She was still surrounded by love.

I asked Amanda if she wanted to take a couple of longer trips with me, and she said, "Sure, why not?" It was so much fun to travel with her. We flew to Paris and lounged on the lawn across from the Eiffel Tower on a perfect summer's day. I needed to be in Atlanta for work, so I went alone. Amanda flew into the city and surprised me. It was so great to see her. We went to Park City, Utah, and saw the sights. Sometimes we just drove out to the mountains northeast of Los Angeles and hiked through the forests.

Tokyo is one of my favorite cities on earth. I love the people and culture. We flew to Japan and went whiskey-tasting and toured a bunch of little bars. It was so much fun. I took Amanda to the most romantic restaurant I knew in Tokyo, this incredible underground eatery that serves twelve-course dinners, and we talked more deeply about what we both wanted in life. When the main course was served, she grabbed her fork, speared together a couple pieces of food, and handed the fork across the table to me to taste. She'd built the perfect mouthful, perfectly delicious. Casually she remarked, "You know I love you, because I just gave you my first bite."

"Wait a minute," I said, unable to stifle a grin. "What did you just say?"

She reddened and opened her mouth as if to clarify.

"No," I said quickly. "You don't have to repeat it. Because I love you too."

That was the first time we had told each other "I love you." On her part, the words had slipped out innocently, impulsively, purely. I had no problem saying them in return with full intention. I should have said them first. We were both at that place in our hearts.

"I see us having a home together someday," I added.

"I do too," she murmured.

"And I'll go even further," I said. "I see us being incredible parents someday." The move felt risky, but I didn't want to hide what was in my heart. I wanted Amanda to know how serious I was about her.

She smiled. "I feel the same way."

WHEN AMANDA'S MOTHER HAD DIED, THE FAMILY HAD scattered her ashes in San Diego off a little rock pier near a beach restaurant. She and her mom used to go there and have tacos and beer. Amanda told me all about their special place. After her mother's passing, the location reminded her of good times. The waves roll in to this little cove and splash against the rocks, and every time Amanda went there she could sense her mom's presence and remember her cleverness. In her mind's eye, she could see her mother's giant smile and almost hear her mischievous laugh anew.

"What's your favorite place in the world?" I asked Amanda once.

"The beach," she said quickly. Then she thought a moment and clarified, "Actually, that one beach I told you about. That's where I feel the most at home. When my mom first died, I knew I'd have to do so much of life without her. That terrified me. But whenever I go to that beach, I feel her strength. She gives me the confidence to go on."

Months went by, and I grew to love Amanda's family. She grew to love mine. My father and her father talked in Spanish together one time, and that's all it took for their bromance to begin. Christmas was approaching, and we planned a trip to Mexico between Christmas and New Year's to celebrate the holidays. Together with friends, we flew to Cabo San Lucas and played in the sun, walked on the beach, rode four-wheelers in the sand, and enjoyed the fireworks shows that the resort hosts.

Everything was so romantic in Cabo, so perfect, so beautiful, and I wondered if Amanda was thinking that I might propose to her there. But I didn't. Not just then. Instead I said, "It would be cool to spend New Year's Day with your mom at the beach. We could go to San Diego and visit your mom's site and say hi to her."

"That would be cool," Amanda said.

On January 1, 2020, we walked out to the rocks in that same cove where the waves roll in and splash. The blue sky was stitched with a lace of white clouds, and I said, "You mean so much to me, Amanda. Remember when you said it really bums you out because all these happy things are happening to you, but your mom is not here to see them? Well, I figured we could bring a memory to her."

She nodded, then glanced at me, her head tilted slightly to one side, like she wasn't sure what was coming next. I pointed across the way, and just then my mother and Amanda's father could be seen walking toward us, holding a tiny box.

"What's going on?" Amanda asked, then she called to them, "What are you guys doing here?"

"I wanted us to be surrounded by family today," I said, answering for them. My mom and Amanda's dad came close to us and handed me the box, then the two took a few paces back from us so nobody could hear what I said next except Amanda. I dropped to one knee.

"Would you marry me?" I said.

Amanda looked shocked. But she was also smiling. "Yes," she said. "Of course."

The box held a ring. Amanda slid it on the fourth finger of her left hand. Our friends showed up (I'd arranged it earlier) and they celebrated with us on the sand. Back in Cabo, I had called her dad and asked for his permission. I'm old school like that. He was thrilled. My dad couldn't make it to the beach, but he knew the engagement was happening and gave us his blessing too.

Amanda and I started planning our wedding ceremony. Everything was progressing smoothly, then COVID-19 hit. The world shut down, and nobody was gathering anywhere anymore. So we postponed plans for the ceremony until we could do it right. Amanda's dad moved onto our property, too, so we could all be around each other. Amanda and

I quarantined together in our house, and we had meals together and went for walks in the evening, and I brought her flowers every chance I could. It didn't seem like quarantining, being together with her. We went for walks on the beach. The quarantining brought us closer together. But another big surprise was right around the corner.

ON FATHER'S DAY 2020, WE HELD A BARBECUE FOR HER dad and my dad at our house. When the meal was over and the festivities were quieting down, Amanda called me into the bathroom. She was late, so she'd decided to take a pregnancy test, and she wanted me there so we could see the results together. After the stick changed color, she didn't look at it directly but quickly snapped a picture of the results with a Polaroid camera. Then we both stared at the picture. In that tantalizing Polaroid way, slowly the details of the picture emerged.

Two lines.

Amanda started to cry. I was beside myself with excitement. We sketched the news onto a little cardboard sign but didn't show anyone at first. Instead, we walked out into the backyard and gathered everyone for a group photo. Amanda and I stood in the back of the group, then held up the sign quickly as the group picture was snapped. We gathered our fathers and showed them the photo.

"Look closely," Amanda said.

Both our fathers spotted the sign. They laughed. Then they cried. We were all emotional together. We brought my mom over so she could share in the exciting news too. It was a Father's Day to remember forever.

Then the journey began. I wish I could describe the anticipation of being a father, how incredible and exhilarating that feeling is. Amanda and I were quarantined at home for much of the pregnancy, and it was a beautiful run. I made sure Amanda had everything she needed, and I worked to make sure she was laughing every day, able to just enjoy each beautiful moment of this special time.

The only sad part was that due to quarantining, I wasn't allowed to be in the ultrasound room with her when she had her appointments. I could take her to the hospital and stay in the hallway, FaceTiming her. We both wore masks, and near the seven-week ultrasound appointment, Amanda held her phone close to her belly. We both heard our baby's heartbeat for the first time. That felt like a milestone. It's no exaggeration to say our entire lives changed with the rhythm of that little life. Something woke up in me that I'd never seen or recognized before. A new level of pride, joy, love. No matter how much attention I gave to my career, or how much success I experienced in it, nothing would ever be as fulfilling as hearing our child's heartbeat for the first time.

From then on, I wanted to hear it all the time. I bought a portable ultrasound machine for the house. Amanda just laughed at me. She didn't like applying gel on her stomach all the time, but she'd do it every so often. We both loved hearing this song of life.

A few weeks later, we held a gender reveal party at our house. Our backyard is large and airy, but even so, a party was no easy thing to pull off during COVID-19. All the guests remained outside and followed guidelines and took necessary precautions to ensure everybody's safety. Our home was thoroughly sanitized before and after the party, and every guest was tested before and after the gathering. The backyard was decorated with balloons and streamers, and we set up a comment box so people could help us pick a name.

We all ate barbecue and tacos and cake, and when it came time for the big reveal, that's when the real fun started. We'd arranged for a helicopter to fly over the house. Everybody looked up into the sky, with hearts wide open. I gathered Amanda in my arms, and we gazed upward, anticipating a moment that would live in our hearts forever. A skydiver leaped from the helicopter. Colored smoke from a canister on the skydiver's ankle would indicate the gender. Down he came.

It's a girl!

Everybody clapped and cheered as pink smoke colored the sky. The skydiver's chute billowed out and snapped into place. Amanda and I embraced and kissed. Slowly, the skydiver descended into our backyard. We were parents of a daughter. A new season had officially begun. Amanda told me later she was feeling so much gratitude and peace during the gender reveal. A wave of calmness flowed through her body.

The pregnancy progressed, and friends and family soon held a virtual baby shower for her. One night, Amanda's mother appeared to her in a clear and symbolic dream, celebrating along with us. Amanda felt so supported and excited.

About two weeks before our due date, Amanda and I had one last getaway together, this time to a resort in Ventura. At lunch, we were researching names and came across Nakano Takeko, a historical Japanese female warrior. Well educated, honorable, and beautiful, Nakano Takeko lived and fought bravely in the 1800s. We both agreed the name sounded cool, powerful, and strong. I could envision our daughter going on her first date. A boy would ask, "What does your name mean?" and she would say with a laugh, "Female samurai. Don't mess with me."

So that's what we chose. Nakano. Partially for the strength the name signifies, and partially to commemorate our trip to Japan, the one where Amanda and I first told each other we loved each other and could envision ourselves as parents together. Our daughter's middle name, Oceana, emerged as a tribute to Amanda's mother. We wanted our daughter to remember her heritage and also to have a strong connection with the ocean. Nakano Oceana Valderrama. Everything was so peaceful on our getaway to Ventura. Just the wind and the sun and the water and us. The anticipation grew, and one day we blinked, and it was nearly time.

We were all at home the week Amanda was due, and one afternoon out of the blue a beautiful white crane landed in our backyard. The bird was tall and sleek and gorgeous, and I'd never seen anything like it, even though I'd lived in the house for years. Amanda and I walked out to the crane, but it didn't fly away. It just looked at us with a steady, wise stare.

A few days later, on February 13, we went to Cedars-Sinai Medical Center for our last checkup. We rode the elevator up to the labor and delivery floor, where we hadn't been yet. When the elevator opened, directly on the wall across from us was a glass case with a kimono inside. On the kimono was printed a white crane. We didn't know what it all meant, but we took it as a positive sign that everything about Nakano would align perfectly.

We spent Valentine's Day at home. February 14. Everything was quiet. That night we went to bed early. A few hours later, Amanda's water broke. It was 1:43 a.m. If you used a pager back in the 1990s, then you know "143" was code for "I love you." Quickly we gathered everything we needed and rushed to the hospital. Amanda had contractions in the delivery room all that morning and far into the afternoon. This time, I was allowed to be in the same room with her.

I took my job as coach extremely seriously. She was doing all the heavy lifting, but I was there to give Amanda support. At one point during the contractions, I was holding her left leg with my left hand and the back of her neck with my right hand. Like the world's biggest dummy, I was talking over the doctor, trying to do "the most," as we say in the streets, instructing Amanda what to do with her abs. (As if I knew anything about delivering a baby.) Just in case I needed one more indication of how absolutely amazing and gracious Amanda is, during a particularly intense bout of contractions, I asked if she wanted some music to go with the mood. We needed a soundtrack. The doctor and nurses looked at each other like, "Is he serious?" I asked Amanda what song she would like to hear. Amanda stared at me hard, her sense of humor fierce and undaunted, and said, "'Push It.'" We laughed as much as we could in the moment, and Amanda kept at it. She pushed it real good. She's an incredible champion.

At 4:04 p.m., February 15, 2021, Nakano Oceana emerged into the world, all six pounds, six ounces of her, pure and wonderful. Amanda and I both took her to our chests skin to skin right away, which they say helps build a bond, and it was like some kind of different program woke up in my brain. I have never felt so alive. There was one more miracle to the day too.

February 15 was Amanda's mother's birthday.

WHEN OUR DAUGHTER ENTERED OUR LIVES, OUR world completely melted. Sure, there were some long nights. We had to figure out life with a newborn, what it meant to put her to bed, what she was asking for when she was crying. But mostly it was pure joy. As a toddler, Nakano is gentle, easygoing, and fun. She has the kind of personality that makes Amanda and I say to each other, "What about having three more children?"

I noticed that the smallest tasks seemed to take on new meaning. Bath time. Nibbling on her tiny feet. Snuggling with her together on the couch. Soon she developed opinions of her own. She didn't like it if we wore sunglasses. She hated it if I had any facial stubble; only a clean cheek would do. Nakano soon became the sunlight of our every day. She shines on all of us. We might be driving somewhere on a cloudy winter day, but if she's in the car with us, it feels like springtime. Any time she hears music, she's smiling and clapping and can't stop. I can't believe how much joy this child has brought to us.

My relationship with Amanda has deepened too. A baby brings more work into a household. We find that we listen to each other more and work to understand each other better. Once the restrictions for COVID-19 lifted and I was back on set every day, it meant that I wasn't able to invest the same amount of time at home as I'd been doing. So I got two trailers on set at *NCIS*, one for me and one for Amanda and Nakano, any time they want to visit. Amanda decorated the inside of the second trailer like a baby's room. They often come to the set and eat lunch with me. We play for a while, then Nakano takes a nap, then they head home for the afternoon.

Even with the added responsibilities and more complicated scheduling, Amanda and I are still very much in love. Our love is based on commitment, even more than feelings, and I never want to take our relationship for granted. The promise we made to each other from the start was to create a lifelong link between us and to create a secure environment where children can thrive. I want Amanda to feel heard and listened to, and despite my schedule, I want us to do as many activities together as possible. I have a project coming up where I'll be doing a lot of horseback riding, sword fighting, and flamenco dancing. Amanda and I are set to take classes together so we can enjoy the same activities.

We were both blessed with wonderful sets of parents. Yet we know we are not the same as our parents, and we don't have to repeat their stories. We are part of their stories, but we are the architects of our own. The book of our life together is being written, and we are both holding the same pen.

CHAPTER 12

Awards and Rewards

H ey, Wilmer, there's this Walt Disney animated film being created. It's top secret, and I can't send you the whole script yet.
But they're interested in you, and you would play a father of a big
family." Not long after Amanda and I became a couple, I received
this phone call from agent Brittany Balbo, co-head of United Talent
Agency's endorsements and voiceover department. Then she added,
"Just one important question. Can you sing?"

"No problem," I said. "I grew up singing."

She described one of the scenes I'd be in and as much as possible
about the movie, which sounded fantastic but didn't provide much
information. The entire project was highly secretive.

"Oh," she added, "and I can tell you that Lin-Manuel Miranda is
writing the music."

"Lin-Manuel?" I said. "I love him. I'm in."

It was that simple. I'd known Lin-Manuel for years. Back in 2005,
he wrote the music and lyrics and starred in the Broadway stage production of *In the Heights*. The show captured the heart of how it looked
and felt to live in the predominantly Latino neighborhood of Upper

Manhattan called Washington Heights. Every character in the play dreams of a better life.

When the play debuted, the Latino community came out in full support. Even then, Lin-Manuel didn't really need our help. His play was amazing, and the appeal crossed over from the Latino community to all people and cultures. The world discovered Lin-Manuel's prodigious iconography through his production of *In the Heights*, and from then on, the world was hooked. I remember sitting in the theater, completely mesmerized. We were seeing a modern-day Mozart at work. He'd reinvented Broadway and created so many memorable moments in that play. Afterward when he and I met, Lin-Manuel impressed me as super humble, a thoughtful man who never forgot his roots. For *In the Heights*, he won two Tonys as well as a Grammy.

Lin-Manuel and I stayed in touch, and I came to know him as a wise and bighearted performer who helped many people both onstage and behind the scenes. In an era when the Latino culture struggled to make ripples, Lin-Manuel was cannonballing into the deep end, making a huge splash.

In 2015, he went on to create the Broadway sensation *Hamilton*, a phenomenally creative take on the life of American founding father Alexander Hamilton. It's no exaggeration to say that audiences everywhere loved *Hamilton*. This show received near-universal acclaim, winning a staggering eleven Tony Awards and the 2016 Pulitzer Prize for Drama. I mean, the man is a legend. To join him on this storytelling journey would be the ride of a lifetime. To unite forces with Lin-Manuel was a slam-dunk decision for me. Everything he creates moves people.

I went and read for the part, then sent an audio recording of me singing. COVID-19 had just hit, so few things were being done in person, and any face-to-face meeting was highly controlled according to ever-shifting state regulations.

The movie's name intrigued me right from the start. *Encanto*, a Spanish word meaning "enchantment," or a sort of delighted, magical charm. Wonder upon wonders, the movie was set in Colombia! My mother's home country featured on-screen in the United States—how cool is that?

I loved the plot. *Encanto* is the story of an extraordinary, magical family, the Madrigals, who live in a benevolent thinking house that moves. The Madrigal family magic blesses their entire town, yet their magic is threatened from the start of the movie.

Complicating things, each Madrigal family member—except one—receives a special power on one of their early childhood birthdays. The mother, Julieta, heals people with the food she cooks. A sister, Luisa, has superhuman strength and can lift pianos, donkeys, barrels, a church, and even a bridge. Another sister, Isabela, is the golden child who causes flowers to bloom and creates elaborate natural decorations anywhere she goes. Aunt Pepa controls the weather with her emotions. Cousin Delores has super hearing. Cousin Camilo can shape-shift into any person he wants to be. Cousin Bruno can see the future, but he doesn't live with the family anymore, and it's forbidden to talk about him, which is one of the plot points. Mirabel's youngest cousin, Antonio, receives his gift near the start of the movie on his fifth birthday. He can communicate with animals.

Only the quirky fifteen-year-old daughter, Mirabel, receives no gift, one of the big mysteries that's raised near the start. When Mirabel discovers that the family is losing their magic, she embarks on a quest to find the truth—and to save her family, the town, and their enchanted house.

I landed the role of Agustín Madrigal, husband of Julieta and father of Isabela, Luisa, and Mirabel. Since my character married into the family, he has no magical powers of his own. Yet he's empathetic, considerate, and full of good intentions. He loves being surrounded by exceptional people, and because he's a bit accident prone, he often benefits from his wife's healing powers. On-screen in animated form, Agustín looks tall and slender. He wears a suit and has a thin mustache. He gets stung by a swarm of bees, and his pocket watch is stolen, which becomes an important piece of the plot.

It wasn't easy to make a movie during COVID-19, but everybody got really creative and worked hard. We didn't interact with other characters, instead recording parts over Zoom, or coming in to the studio alone (triple masked), to play our parts. When I sang, Lin-Manuel guided my harmonies from a distance. Jared Bush, Charise Castro Smith, and Byron Howard directed the film, and we became good friends. They continually encouraged us to play our roles envisioning the warmest family connections, which says something about how powerful the movie became. Our hearts were enmeshed together with every word.

The movie was made during a time when America needed much healing. COVID-19 was physically keeping us apart. The ensuing culture wars were dividing perspectives. The storyline of *Encanto* helps transcend culture and bring people back together. It shows how all people can be moved by a powerful story that connects people of all heritages. Every person knows what it feels like to be happy or sad, scared or embarrassed. The end result was that the movie became a great example of what could happen when we just accept one another and are allowed to run free.

The character of the grandmother (*abuela*) and her storyline hit me most powerfully. Alma Madrigal is her name, and as a young woman, she must flee her hometown with her husband, Pedro, and their three babies. It's the time of the Thousand Days' War, a historical civil conflict that happened from 1899 to 1902, and the family escapes the oppression, along with some of their neighbors. But as they cross a river, armed enemy horsemen catch up with them. Tenderly, Pedro says goodbye to Alma and his children, then runs back toward the horsemen to defend his family and fellow citizens, ultimately sacrificing his life. Now a grieving widow, Alma continues forward with their babies in search of a better life.

Lin-Manuel wrote a song called *"Dos Oruguitas"* ("two caterpillars"), sung by Sebastián Yatra in Spanish and played during one of the most emotional moments in the movie, the scene where Pedro lays down his life for his wife and children. In the narrative of the song, two caterpillars fall in love, but the world changes and they must build their futures alone. The song absolutely soars with emotion, and I knew it to be the theme of far too many people who have come to a new country in search of a better future. Hardship separates them from loved ones, sometimes by death, other times by distance. Their future indeed turns out to be better, but it's bittersweet. In moving toward opportunity, they must leave something valued behind. Any time I hear that song, it makes me tear up.

Encanto premiered at the famed El Capitan Theatre in Hollywood in November 2021, with limited seating due to COVID-19. Cases were declining in Los Angeles by then, and moviegoers were cautiously returning to theaters for the Thanksgiving and holiday season. Still, outdoor gatherings were the norm, and many people didn't feel comfortable in theaters yet.

I brought Amanda, my mother, my sisters, and nephew, Christian, to the premiere. Nakano was a baby and stayed at home with a sitter. The film opens with a song sung by famed musician Carlos Vives, the Frank Sinatra of Colombia and one of the most influential and bestselling Latin music artists of all time. My mother instantly recognized his voice. In the opening scenes, kids are drinking coffee in a humorous moment, flavorful arepas are referenced, and vivid colors are displayed. These were all things we'd grown up with. Through the dimmed light of the theater, I glanced at my mother and sisters and nephew and saw smiles on every face. This was the first time I'd seen the movie all put together, and I was delighted to witness how it captivated everybody's attention.

When it concluded, I knew we'd made something special. The story and performances were strong and vibrant. The songs were spectacular. We hoped everybody would love this movie.

Even so, I don't think we were quite prepared for the amazingly positive reaction the movie received. Despite COVID-19, the movie did well in theaters all across the United States. At the end of the month, it premiered in Bogotá, Colombia. It was released a month later on Disney+ so everybody could see it at home. In early January, it was released in China. Reviewers gave it big thumbs-up, and the consensus was that *Encanto* was a beautiful, culturally relevant movie that was fun for the whole family. *Encanto* went viral and became the most-watched film of 2022. It was Disney's first animated feature with an all-Latin cast, and to date, it's grossed more than $256 million worldwide.

Then came the awards.

Encanto won a Golden Globe for Best Animated Feature Film, three Grammys, and a score of other awards. It was nominated for three Oscars: Best Animated Feature, Best Original Score, and Best Original Song for "*Dos Oruguitas.*"

Amanda and I went to the Oscar Nominees Night, which happens a few weeks before the awards ceremony, and a spokesperson from *The Hollywood Reporter* asked me how it felt to have *Encanto* so well represented. I stood on the red carpet with cameras flashing around me and said, "When you make a film that invites people to celebrate a culture and how much you can see yourself in another family, it's a beautiful thing to see how many this film has touched. We knew it was special, but we had no idea how much people needed this movie." It truly felt wonderful to have this movie be celebrated on the highest levels possible.

Life continued between the nominations and the awards ceremonies. Meanwhile, Amanda, Nakano, and I landed on the front cover of both the English and Spanish versions of *Parents* magazine. Inside, they did a beautiful story and photo spread on us, and in the article we talked about the joys of life with Nakano, the sleep deprivation of life with a newborn, and how Nakano made our life feel so complete. Nakano celebrated her first birthday on February 15, 2022, and we held a quiet celebration with family and friends.

On March 27, 2022, Amanda and I went to the Oscar ceremonies. They're considered by many to be the most important night in the entertainment industry, a truly big deal. Amanda always looks amazing, even if she's just wearing jeans and a T-shirt at home without any makeup. But for this night she had a team of specialists come in to do her hair and makeup. I wore a deep-green, velvet Dolce and Gabbana tuxedo, and she wore a stunning floor-length black evening gown, also by Dolce and Gabbana. On that evening it was no exaggeration to say she looked as glamorous as any iconic Hollywood star.

At the awards ceremony, *Entertainment Tonight* cohosts Nischelle Turner and Kevin Frazier stopped us on the red carpet on our way inside. Both are people of color. I knew Nischelle from her days as a journalist at CNN, and I knew Kevin from my guest appearance on *NCIS: Hawaii.* Nischelle brushed my shoulders with a laugh, and I said, "Look at you. Who let us in this place?" And Kevin said, "We've been saying that all night."

We talked a bit about the Latin flavor of the Oscars that year, then with cameras rolling I said, "This is a moment that will last us forever. When I first came to the United States, I was just a kid standing two blocks from here, and somebody was getting a star on the Hollywood Walk of Fame. I couldn't see who it was through all the people, but I told my dad, 'One day I'm going to have a star. I'm going to have an Oscar. And I'm going to have an Emmy.' My dad nodded and said,

'Okay, *mijo*, you can do that.' Tonight, for my dad to know that we're at the Oscars, with a film that speaks to him . . ." Here my eyes grew misty, but I composed myself and continued. "I don't want to start crying. But this is America, you know. This is why our country is that land known as the land of opportunity. Every single one of us, with our ethnicities and backgrounds, makes this possible."

Inside the auditorium, we found our seats and the show began. "*Dos Oruguitas*" was one of the featured songs for the night, sung by Sebastián Yatra. The song didn't win in its category, but Sebastian melted everybody's heart through his performance.

When it came time for the award for Best Animated Feature, Lily James, who'd played in the 2015 version of *Cinderella*; Naomi Scott, who'd played Princess Jasmine in the 2019 version of *Aladdin*; and Halle Bailey, who was set to join the club in her portrayal of Ariel in the 2023 version of *The Little Mermaid*, read the nominees: *Encanto*, *Flee*, *Luca*, *The Mitchells vs. the Machines*, and *Raya and the Last Dragon*. And the Oscar went to:

Encanto!

It was an incredible feeling. This movie was the little engine that could. A magical town in Colombia was now being honored on the biggest stage on the planet. Directors Jared Bush and Byron Howard and producers Yvett Merino and Clark Spencer took the stage to receive the award. .

Before the ceremonies concluded, Amanda and I needed to duck out early, because I had to be on a red-eye to New York for a TV appearance on *CBS Mornings* early the next day and on *The Late Show with Stephen Colbert* later. It had been a beautiful evening, with all the diverse voices that were heard and all the awards received and so well deserved. COVID-19 was lifting, and everybody needed to get out and feel the new energy. The fact that a terrific movie with brown voices and brown faces won an Oscar was a high point in the history of Hollywood. As an American culture, we had been united in spirit with the Family Madrigal. We had all come a long way. That's what needs to be remembered from the 2022 Oscars.

When I landed in New York early the next morning, with no time to go to my hotel first, I took a car straight to the studio. On *CBS News*, I talked about the Oscars and gave a few teasers about an upcoming episode of *NCIS* where I was guesting on *NCIS: Hawaii*.

Later in the day, with Stephen Colbert, the first question he asked, with a wink—alluding to the memorable moment between Will Smith and Chris Rock—was if I'd seen anything unusual at the Oscars. I mentioned I'd been in the car on the way to the airport and missed everything, to which Stephen replied, "Now at least you can say 'I was in no way involved in that situation.'" Which made everybody laugh.

Quickly, we moved on to discuss *Encanto*, and he asked me about Nakano, if she was old enough yet to have heard the soundtrack. I remarked that Amanda and I had played it for her when the movie released, and she'd been asking for it ever since. Nakano, at just over a year old, would stand up, clap her hands, and do a little dance to the songs.

"But her moves looked awfully close to a twerk," I joked, "and it's a little too early for that. So we were saying 'No more *Encanto* soundtrack' for now." That got a good laugh too.

Stephen asked me a few questions about *NCIS*, and we showed a clip of the upcoming special. We were all moving onward.

I HAD MENTIONED TO THE REPORTERS ON THE RED carpet how I'd promised my dad that someday I would have a star on the Hollywood Walk of Fame and a place at the Oscars and Emmys. I've never won an Emmy personally, although *That '70s Show* was nominated for sixteen Primetime Emmys and won once. But I had the honor of being a presenter at the 2021 Emmy Awards. Along with my sister from another mother Vanessa Lachey, I presented the award for Outstanding Supporting Actor in a Limited or Anthology Series or Movie. I was proud to share a stage with many of my colleagues. Evan Peters, who plays Detective Colin Zabel on *Mare of Easttown*, took home the award. Presenting an Emmy isn't the same as personally receiving one, but I was honored to do so. An Emmy win in my dad's honor will happen someday.

After work one evening, I was driving home, thinking about how actual awards are nice to receive but that accolades of the entertainment industry can emerge in lots of ways. Mostly, I'm not concerned about awards. I'm focused on doing my job, showing up day in and day out, delivering the best performances I can give. The job itself is my biggest reward.

I'm also honored to help broaden the industry for fellow performers. Later that evening at home, I was reading in the *Los Angeles Times* how the Academy of Motion Picture Arts and Sciences reported that even after inducting its 2021 class, only 33 percent of its members were women and only 19 percent were from underrepresented ethnic or racial communities. Another study showed that from 2015 to 2019, only 8 percent of movie executives, 13 percent of TV executives, and 10 percent of agents and executives in the country's top three talent agencies were people of color.[1]

I've set about to help change that, sometimes in smaller ways, sometimes in larger. My production company, now called WV Entertainment, has developed a wide variety of programming over the past twenty years, mostly showcasing diverse and underrepresented voices. We've done everything from animation and scripted series to documentary-style reality shows and podcasts. We're going even bigger today. The infrastructure is in place to tell the stories we want to tell. Currently, I have a staff who handles the day-to-day operations while I focus on vision, connections, and leading the company. The door has cracked wide open for shows that amplify marginalized voices. A lot of what we do is kept under wraps until it happens, but suffice to say, some amazing projects are in the works.

Together with my business partner John Pollak, a former executive at NBCUniversal, we created another structure, Allied Management Group, which acts as a bridge for writers, showrunners, and directors from Latin America. We help place these new storytellers into Hollywood. Basically, we're an agency for Latino voices, helping other talented people break into the industry. We're gathering steam, and we have big plans for the future.

In summer 2021, with everybody quarantining, I did a series of interviews on Instagram Live chats called *Six Feet Apart,* where I'd talk to the people on the front lines. They didn't get to go home and rest and stay safe when everybody else was quarantining. Doctors. Nurses. Delivery drivers. Childcare workers. Grocery workers. Restaurant workers. These people were often overlooked during COVID-19, and I wanted us all to understand what they were going through and for us to develop empathy and, most importantly, show up for our essential workers too.

I teamed up with iHeartRadio, the number one podcast publisher around the world, and this idea morphed into a weekly podcast called *Essential Voices with Wilmer Valderrama.* Some of the conversations have been very sobering, when we understand what people go through. In each show, the conversation leads to a roundtable discussion with a think tank of activists and experts who discuss issues, explore areas needing change, and visualize how things could be different.

A partnership with iHeart was born in the process. Now I'm a stakeholder in My Cultura Network. Our company, WV Sounds, signed a major deal where we produce podcasts for Latinx voices, helping to amplify marginalized people. Ultimately, I hope to strengthen the connections between us all.

SHORTLY BEFORE *ENCANTO* DEBUTED, I RECEIVED A phone call from Kurtwood Smith. "Hey, let's go to dinner," was all he said. So Amanda and I went out with Kurtwood and his wife, Joan Pirkle. We caught up on what we'd all been doing, then Kurtwood said, "You'll never guess what. They're talking about doing a new show where Debra Jo Rupp and I play the grandparents of Eric and Donna's daughter, Leia. It's all pretty hush-hush right now, but it if becomes real, I'll let you know. I'd like for you to show up for a few episodes and play Fez again."

I had to think about that one. I'd retired Fez and moved on. But a few months went by, and Kurtwood texted me. "It's real. It's happening. And Bonnie and Terry are back, producing it."

I love Kurtwood and Debra Jo and all our cast members, and I'd do anything for them. I owe so much to Bonnie and Terry Turner. They had produced *That '70s Show*, and it is not only love I feel toward them; it's a deep appreciation. They had discovered me. I owed them. Plus, they were simply amazing producers.

The new sitcom was titled *That '90s Show* and set to premiere on Netflix on January 19, 2023. I talked to Ashton, Mila, Topher, and Laura, and they were all set to play cameos. Gregg Mettler was set to be the showrunner. He'd joined the writing staff of *That '70s Show* during season four and had stayed until the last episode. He's always great. The Turners' daughter, Lindsey, was coming on board to develop the show. It was truly going to happen.

Set in 1995, the show picks up one generation removed from *That '70s Show*. The gang's all grown up now. Eric and Donna's daughter,

Leia, played by Callie Haverda, comes to Point Place, Wisconsin, for the summer and stays with Red and Kitty, her grandparents. She befriends a new group of teens, and the fun begins.

Opening up that chapter of my life again felt strangely emotional for me. We'd had such an iconic run with *That '70s Show*, nobody wanted to mess with that, and we all thought we'd closed it up tight in 2006. I had retired the Fez accent and voice. In the years since, I didn't care how much anybody begged me, I didn't do it anymore. Fez was gone.

But the overall story question of *That '90s Show* intrigued me. I wondered where all these characters had ended up. Could there truly be a more mature version of Fez? If so, where would he be now? What would he be doing? The writers called me, and we began to work together, helping shape a new, grown-up Fez. The answers we came up with delighted me. Fez had become the Paul Mitchell of Wisconsin. He's a successful businessman, running a chain of high-end hair salons called Chez Fez. I was happy that Fez was okay. But even more than that, I resonated with his story. Fez was an immigrant who came to the United States and succeeded in achieving the American dream. This was a great story arc for him. I was thrilled to see that Fez was doing just fine.

During rehearsals, we prepared for more shows than the pilot. Ten episodes had been ordered. I focused on building momentum, stepping into the role again and letting Fez live and breathe once more. The producers asked me for input about how Fez should make his grand entrance. We talked about his hair, how it would be exaggerated in the front and totally '90s. They indicated he would drive a blue Miata. So I said, "Let's make this as epic as possible. Let's put him in white jeans. Plus, I think he should be lying on the hood of the Miata for his opening shot." Everything fell into place.

On the day of the first live taping, about three hundred audience members packed Sunset Bronson Studios. The pilot starts with Kitty and Red dancing in the kitchen. Everybody cheered loudly for them. Eric shows up next. He's at the front door with his daughter, Leia, bringing the family home for the Fourth of July holiday. Everybody cheered again. Donna shows up a few moments later, carrying in the luggage. Again, the audience clapped and whistled. New characters were featured throughout, and they all delivered their lines flawlessly, getting big laughs. The writing was tight and punchy. A few scenes later, Kelso bursts on the stage, and the audience hit the roof for him. A few moments later, Jackie bursts in. True to character, she is upset at Kelso, and the audience responded wildly. A new actor, Andrea Anders, appears as Sherri, the Formans' new neighbor who's dating Fez but wondering if their relationship can go the distance. She delivered every line flawlessly.

Fez is shown in a quick preview shot at the end of the pilot, but he doesn't make his grand entrance until the conclusion of episode two. I had humble expectations for how Fez might be received by audience members. All he does is make a quick appearance at the end of the show where he was set to say, "Hello, sugar pants." (The line was eventually rewritten for the version that made it onto TV.) Again for that taping, the studio was packed. Tommy Chong makes an appearance early in the episode. The audience all cheered. The episode continues with one of the plotlines being Sherri wondering if she should break up with my character.

From where the live audience views the stages in the studio, people often can't see everything that's happening all at once. Sometimes stages are covered by curtains. Audience members can look at video monitors, which sometimes lets them see more of what's happening. When it came time for me to come out, the garage and driveway areas were covered. Stagehands brought me in through the back of the garage under secrecy. I took my place, lying on the hood of the Miata on my side, with my left hand holding my head up, and my knees way too far from each other, as only Fez could do.

Suddenly a loud, passionate roar erupted from the stands. The exuberance took me off guard, because I didn't know what the audience was seeing and reacting to. I found out later that they were seeing Fez in the monitors, as I was getting ready to say my line. The roar only got louder. People were yelling, screaming, clapping. I was trying to stay in character. I looked offstage and saw Andrea's eyes getting teary. I waited for the level of cheering to drop slightly so I could deliver my line. Finally the cheering fell just enough. I delivered the line. The director yelled "Cut!" and the audience went crazy. The stagehands pulled up the curtain, and I could see the audience now. They were going nuts.

I choked up as it hit me: this love was all for Fez. Rarely does this happen for an actor. You play a character for years, and you know he's well received, but you don't ever realize what kind of impact a character makes. Audience members were paying tribute to a piece of history, and I found myself starting to do the same. In real life, Fez had been a game changer for me. He introduced me to audiences, and he gave me and my family a far better life than we had ever imagined.

After it debuted, *That '90s Show* was a hit, soaring into Netflix's top five TV English titles within its first week. In its first three days alone after its debut, more than forty-one million hours of the show were watched. Many critics also responded positively. All episodes of season one were released simultaneously on the streamer, and the show was soon picked up for a second season, this time for sixteen episodes.

BUT I HAVE AN EVEN BIGGER JOY. IN FEBRUARY 2023 Nakano celebrated her second birthday. By this point in my life, I'd seen that there are many awards and rewards an actor can receive in this industry. For some, an actor shows up onstage and people cheer, or they dip their hands and feet into cement and people take photos. Others come more subtly, such as the reward of knowing you're bringing other people along with you, or the reward of knowing a character you played over years has sunk into the hearts of viewers. Then there are the personal rewards.

The restrictions for COVID-19 had lifted sufficiently for us to have a huge party for Nakano. All our family members were there, plus many of our friends and their children. We went with a 1970s theme, and the party space was decorated with a mass of magical balloons and funky streamers. We brought in a bouncy house and a piñata, we had dancing under a glittery disco ball, and there was a little slide that let kids glide into a pool of bright white playground balls. Amanda and I both dressed up in fun retro clothes, me wearing a blue denim jumpsuit and Amanda wearing flowers in her hair, white flared jeans, a long-sleeved orange-swirl shirt, and an ultracool fringed vest. Many of the guests and their kids dressed up too.

Near the end of the party, when it came time to cut the cake, we all gathered around Nakano. My dad, who absolutely adores his granddaughter, was a puddle of laughs and tears. My mother and Nakano are besties, and they'd stayed close to each other throughout the evening. Nakano was able to blow out her own candles, and that was the biggest moment for me. With Nakano in my arms, I took the microphone, held it in front of her, and gently instructed her to tell everybody, "Thank you for coming." Nakano got out the words. Such a brilliant girl. Already giving speeches.

There are Oscars and Emmys and stars on the Hollywood Walk of Fame, and then there's strapping your daughter into her car seat and driving her home after a night of fun. There's holding her close in your arms as she sleeps and walking into your house, putting her jammies on, tucking her into bed, and smoothing her hair on her forehead. You'll be there for her in the morning when she wakes up. You and the one you love will be there together. Those are the awards and rewards that can't be topped.

CHAPTER 13

Luck

The place was packed. I'd gone to a Hollywood restaurant for dinner to talk business with a friend. They didn't take reservations, and we quickly saw that all the tables were filled, so we sat at the bar, ordered our food, and waited, our stomachs growling. At last our plated steaks arrived in all their sizzling glory. Seriously, I was one millisecond away from tasting the first mouthwatering bite when a stranger walked up to me from behind, tapped me on the shoulder, and exclaimed, "Torres? That's you, right? Nick Torres!"

I set down my fork and turned around on the barstool. "Yes, that's me."

For the next thirty minutes, the guy talked as quickly as he could. A superfan of *NCIS*, he knew all the ins and outs of the show. He could remember intricate details from episodes I was in years ago. He had theories about the relationships that different characters play out among themselves. He wanted to know everything about each upcoming show that I could possibly tell him.

My steak grew cold. Undoubtedly, I could have excused myself, turned back around to face the bar, and returned to my meal and my business conversation. But in all honesty, I didn't mind the interruption. Regularly I remind myself that I have a great job. The fans are the heart in the artist's body. They keep the heart beating. The reason I'm in show business today is because of the trust and continuous support of the fans.

One word the guy spoke, however, stayed with me for a long while. Whenever I hear this word—and I hear it a lot—it unsettles me. It's just so inaccurate. I wish I could have clarified to him what I thought about this word, because it's actually in his own best interest to understand the truth. But the word takes a while to unpack, and a busy restaurant on a Friday night wasn't the time and place. He asked for an autograph toward the end of our interaction, then he added, "Wow, I can't believe all the things you've done in your career, Wilmer. You are soooooo lucky!"

There was the word that needed debunking.

Luck.

BACK IN 2011, SHORTLY AFTER I'D TURNED THIRTY-ONE, a Latino travel TV show called *Pastport* invited me to return to Venezuela to film an episode of their program. The trip wouldn't be easy. Parts of Venezuela had become even more dangerous than when my family fled the country. We would need a security detail with us at all times. I hadn't returned since I was a kid, so I knew an emotional component would factor into the trip. Cameras would be running all the time, which can sometimes complicate the honesty of an experience.

Yet I jumped at the chance. Tadao came with me, as did my close friend Joe Huff. The producers first flew us to the capital, Caracas, so I could reunite with some of my father's family. For safety's sake, we were told not to let many people know we were coming, but I was able to visit some of my aunts and uncles and cousins, and we had a good time catching up. I have fond childhood memories of my extended family in Venezuela, and now we were able to share several meals and reconnect. "Distance can make someone forget," an aunt said to me.

"I will never forget my roots," I told her.

From Caracas, we traveled by van four-plus hours southwest to Acarigua-Araure, the tiny town where I'd grown up. We connected with my childhood friend Miguel, who warned me about an armed gang called Los Miguelitos operating in the area. They were known for tossing spiked chains in front of moving vehicles to blow the tires. When the vehicle stops, the gang robs everybody inside at gunpoint. If you look wealthy, they kidnap you and hold you for ransom.

"Very dangerous," Miguel said in Spanish.

On the edge of town, we stopped at a church first and prayed. I wasn't worried about the danger of the gangs so much as I wanted the trip to be blessed. And I prayed that the people of Venezuela wouldn't have to live under oppression anymore—either from gangs or their government.

When we arrived in Acarigua-Araure, so many emotions flooded into my soul. I recognized the statue of José Antonio Páez at the roundabout in the town square. He'd been exiled from Venezuela after fighting for freedom. When I was a kid, the statue hadn't been finished, and you could see the inside of the monument. But now he was completed and stood tall and proud, holding two spears, one in each hand. We drove by the same movie theater where I'd seen *RoboCop* all those times. We drove by the beer company, Polar, that sponsored the Little League baseball team I played for. I knew I was home.

My grade school had been notified we were coming, and the students had painted a big Welcome sign in my honor. They were all excited to meet me, and I was happy to meet them too. They held a short commemorative ceremony and gave me an honorary diploma. I talked about how when I was a boy, I had participated in school plays and had taken singing and dancing lessons at the school. It was great to see Venezuela's next generation looking so bright.

We toured the halls and classrooms. There are no glass windows in the school. The walls have openings for fresh air, and the walls and ceilings deliberately aren't sealed to allow for airflow. I breathed in the unchanged scent of the dusty cement blocks, listened to the sound of mango trees swaying in the breeze and wild tropical parrots nearby. The scents and sounds evoked the exact feelings I'd had as a little kid walking from classroom to classroom, wondering about all that the future held.

After we said our goodbyes, we drove toward my childhood home, the house in town that my father had owned. Driving down the street, everything looked the same: small Spanish-style stucco houses, the properties fenced and gated with iron bars, most fences extending to the street, walls gleaming with whitewash in the sunlight. At my old house, oval-shaped openings are cut in the tall fence that surrounds the property. Iron lattice work fills the ovals. Everything looked the same, although time and distance had weathered the paint. Childhood memories streamed over me: birthday parties, riding bicycles and a unicycle (yep, even a unicycle), roller-skating down the street, going to the corner bakery to shop for bread for my mom.

The family that now lived in our old house kindly let us tour the inside. As I wandered from room to room, I became a small child again. It felt like I was watching my mother make soup in the kitchen. I was again helping my father in the backyard where he'd built a pool. The pool was empty now, but everything felt unchanged. In the corner of the backyard was a place where my mom had hand-washed clothes with a tub and a water tap. I turned on the tap. The sound of water gurgling into the tub was exactly the same.

Inside the house again, I climbed the steps to the bedroom that used to be mine. It was still unfinished. The same cinder blocks. The same chipped paint. I looked out through the window and saw the same neighborhood roofs, remembering the endless times when I just hung around and joked with my sisters, or my friends and I climbed to our roof and snacked on sandwiches, talking about all the adventures we would one day have. Tadao nudged me that it was time to go, but I couldn't leave the room just yet. The same custom triangle shelves sat in the corner where I put all my toys. Everywhere I looked were memories. Tadao tapped his watch.

"No, my friend," I said. "Please. One more moment."

I sat on the bed and glanced at the pillow, positioned exactly where I had once laid my head each night. Surely the new owners had replaced the pillow, but it was the same bed frame, positioned the same direction in the room. I closed my eyes. When I had dreamed here years ago, I had dreamed solely in Spanish. But those boyhood dreams had ignited my belief that everything is possible.

Tears began to flow. Not tears of sadness but tears of joy, of pride. Here I was sitting on the same corner of the bed where a young Wilmer had once promised himself that he'd be everything that I had now become. I asked myself: *What can I dream of doing next?*

The answer came in an instant. When I was a child, one television character drew my admiration more than any other. This character gave voice to my people. He championed the cause of the marginalized. He lived a life of adventure and heroics. He held history and the future in one hand and the reins of his beloved horse, Tornado, in the other. I used to watch this same character in black and white on TV in Spanish in my living room. He was my favorite. Whenever I watched him, I knew there could be heroes in the world who looked like me.

Zorro.

"Okay, then," I whispered, not moving from the edge of that bed.

"The same dream will continue. Here I am at age thirty-one, and I vow to honor the child who dreamed big—as well as honor every person of any age and culture who dreams of opportunity. I will do this to honor my heritage. I will do it because I believe this character inspires people to live out their own heroics. I vow that one day soon, I, too, will play on TV the character Zorro."

IF YOU AREN'T FAMILIAR WITH ZORRO, IT'S HARD TO fathom how big he is. He's a global icon who's been around for more than one hundred years. Picture a famous black eye mask, cape, gaucho hat, rapier, and heaps of panache, and you've got the beginnings of Zorro. Around the world, he's more famous than James Bond.

And, oh yeah, he's Latino.

The original story sets this masked crusader in early nineteenth-century California, specifically the Pueblo de los Ángeles. The ethnically diverse inhabitants of the day were throwing off the yoke of Spanish colonization and embracing the Mexican Republic. Zorro was their superhero, the dude who rode in on his horse and fought for their causes, defending the population from oppression.

His name translated into English means "fox." It's an alias. His true name is Don Diego Vega (later called Don Diego de la Vega), and he's actually a man of means and substance and talent, and the character who inspired Batman. The mask. The cape. The underground Batcave. When young Bruce Wayne went to the movie theater with his parents just before they died in the car crash, what movie were they seeing? *The Mark of Zorro.* It's all there in cinematic history.

It's hard to pin a flaw on Zorro. Even a weakness. Superman has his kryptonite. Wonder Woman can't escape from being tied up. The Green Lantern can overcome any obstacle as long as it's not colored yellow. But Zorro? Zorro's the man. He stands firmly against corruption. He champions the poor. Zorro knows how to wield a sword. He's a master marksman. When it comes to horses, he's a veritable professor of the equestrian world. He's brave. Strong. Charming. Witty. Decisive. Loyal. Smart. Moral. Tough. Pick almost any superlative, and it'll stick on Zorro.

But playing Zorro?

How can I describe the level of difficulty in achieving this dream?

It's fair to say every actor in the world would want to play Zorro. The shoes to be filled are huge. Actually, the history of this character is enough to send anybody's dream of playing Zorro crashing right over the cliff.

When I was sitting on my boyhood bed in 2011, vowing anew that one day I'd make good on that specific childhood ambition, I knew that Zorro had been around since 1919, when writer Johnston McCulley dreamed him up in the book *The Curse of Capistrano*. The book was an instant hit, and over the years that followed, Johnston and other authors would write some sixty-five more novels that featured Zorro.

Books were only a start. Meanwhile, Zorro came to life on film in 1920 when Douglas Fairbanks offered the first on-screen portrayal in the silent film *The Mark of Zorro*. Five years later, Douglas reprised the role for the movie *Don Q, Son of Zorro*. An entire decade passed, then Robert Livingston picked up the mantle of Zorro for *The Bold Caballero* in 1936, with Tyrone Power playing him in 1940's *The Mark of Zorro*. Five TV shows about Zorro were also created in that early era, from 1937 to 1949. All of these were American productions. But that was only the beginning of Zorro's fame.

An Italian version of Zorro came out in 1952, then Guy Williams portrayed him in two more American movies in 1958 and 1959, *The Sign of Zorro* and *Zorro, the Avenger*. Guy also played him on a Walt

Disney TV production of Zorro from 1957 to 1959. That was the version of Zorro I remember watching as a kid. While Zorro went on hiatus in America for a while, a staggering twenty-six more international Zorro movies were made from 1961 to 1974—produced in Italy, Spain, Belgium, France, and Mexico. In that era, he became as recognizable as Mickey Mouse or John Wayne.

Back in the USA, Frank Langella breathed new life into Zorro in 1974, then George Hamilton played him in 1981, before Anthony Hopkins portrayed him in 1998's *The Mask of Zorro*, handing the mask to Antonio Banderas in the same movie while making a household name of the movie's costar, Catherine Zeta-Jones. In 2005, Antonio played Zorro in the follow-up *The Legend of Zorro*. The powerhouses TriStar Pictures and Steven Spielberg's Amblin Entertainment had teamed together to produce the first Banderas movie, earning an impressive $250 million. Columbia Pictures jumped in for the second Banderas portrayal, earning $142 million.

The point is this: you don't just knock on somebody's door, cap in hand, and ask to play Zorro. I had sensed that as a kid. I certainly knew that as a thirty-one-year-old. And in the years that followed, the difficulty of playing Zorro was only reinforced to me.

I mean, all these movies and TV shows and books were only one section of Zorro's fame. Overall, the stories of Zorro had been produced in just about every media type known. In his middle era, an animated series for kids called *The New Adventures of Zorro* was seen on Saturday mornings from 1997 to 1998. In 1983, Disney had produced a comedy TV series for adults called *Zorro and Son*. In the 1990s, an international TV series called simply *Zorro* was shown in more than fifty countries for more than four years. A Japanese animated version of Zorro was produced in 1992. There was even an erotic version of Zorro done in 1972, although I refuse to mention the movie's title because I think it was in extremely poor taste.

Along the way, there had been an additional plethora of other books about Zorro, stage productions, video games, and international TV versions. A new Spanish version called *El Zorro: La Espada y la Rosa* had premiered in 2007, and a cool animated series called *Zorro: Generation Z* premiered in 2006. *Zorro: The Musical*, with an original score by the Gipsy Kings, premiered in England in 2008. It received stellar reviews, won awards, and went on to openings in all the world's major theaters: Paris, Moscow, Beirut, Amsterdam, Tokyo, Tel Aviv, and Sao Paolo.

Did I mention the swag? Picture truckloads of Zorro backpacks, lunch boxes, T-shirts, games, comic books, purses, sunglasses, watches, jewelry, perfumes, toys, and commemorative swords and knives. There had even been ice cream parlors and restaurants named in his honor. Zorro's influence around the world was absolutely staggering. But here I was, wanting to be the next Zorro.

This would become my Mount Everest. My seemingly impossible quest.

WHERE MIGHT AN ACTOR EVEN START ON A QUEST like this? You call your agents. So I called and called. From 2011 forward, I checked with my agents every other month or so about playing Zorro, wondering if the time was right, asking if we could find a way. For years, nothing materialized for me. I took other acting parts, and I don't regret any of those roles because they built into me depth and breadth as an actor. But in the back of my head, I was always thinking *Zorro*.

Several times, my agents heard rumors of Zorro being resurrected. They jumped into action, begging studio heads to allow me to take meetings. Sometimes the answer was sure, it couldn't hurt. But other times, the answer wasn't even remotely positive. Some studio heads acted like I wasn't even in the running. They saw me only as Fez. I was too comedic, they said, and I wasn't leading-man material. We showed them my independent work to convince them I was up for the role.

If it ever became available.

Years passed. I never lost sight of my goal. But when I joined *NCIS* in 2016, that further complicated things, because *NCIS* shoots ten months each year. If a Zorro part came up, I'd have to do it during the offseason. That wouldn't be easy.

Meanwhile, I began to see encouraging trends in the entertainment world. Superhero movies began to boom. The Marvel and DC Comics franchises exploded in popularity. It seemed that moviegoers wanted to see as many superheroes in action as they could. Even so, if you were a superhero, chances were good you didn't look like me. But then a few female leads began breaking out. More room was being created.

Finally in 2018, *Black Panther* soared to success. When I watched it in a theater for the first time, I just sat back and grinned. I couldn't believe it. Finally, America had a superhero of color. With Chadwick Boseman starring in the lead role of T'Challa, *Black Panther* would help kick down the door for everybody else. It wasn't that I thought it was wrong to have a long string of white male superheroes; in fact, I grew very fond of them. But as if serendipity had orchestrated this timing itself, *Black Panther* came out in an era when the Black community needed a beacon more than ever. The movie gave the people an image they could believe in. After I saw that movie I thought, *Wow, here we are today: one in every five people in the United States is Latino. Imagine if the Latino community had a similar character who would showcase our culture's value and contribution to humanity. With a Latino superhero, we could see ourselves as we are and as we were. But this time represented positively on-screen—no longer the bad guys. We could say to our children, "This is a hero you can look up to. This is someone you can be."*

After seeing *Black Panther*, I felt a new fire. I upped the pressure. I kept bugging my agents that I needed to be Zorro. They were doing everything they could, making all the calls, but seeing that movie was the watershed moment. Something changed inside me. I knew I could do more. So I made a new plan, even though I confided in very few people about it. I chose to become bolder than ever. I wouldn't wait for the coach to put me in. I would lace up my cleats and charge down the field of my own volition. I would stop waiting for the calls to come to me. I would make my own calls.

Dana Walden, cochair at Disney, was one of the first people I reached out to. She's honest and a straight shooter. I'd known Dana for years, since back when she'd been the CEO of Fox Television Group. She's always been a big sister to me and has always listened. Even so, I was nervous. Before I called her, I wrote out my thoughts on paper. My notes weren't long. But I wanted to keep on track. I wanted her to know exactly what it meant to me and my community.

"Hey, Dana," I said over the phone. "I have this crazy idea. Can I run it by you?"

"Always," she said.

"I need you to tell me if I'm on to something or if I'm full of crap."

"Okay, I'm all ears," she said.

I cleared my throat. "Here's what I'm thinking. I'm at a place in my career as an actor and activist where I see an enormous need not only for accurate representation of Latinos on-screen, but for a reset of our country's values as a whole. Marvel helped do that for the Black community with *Black Panther*. But no one has done that yet specifically for the Latino community, even though we're our nation's second-largest ethnic group. As contributors to the country and as consumers of entertainment, Latinos can be highly influential. Right now, there are more than sixty-two million Latinos in the United States, up 19 percent since 2010. We represent a large piece of the population. Yet only a small percentage of stories on-screen feature positive portrayals of Latinos or Latino leads. So I have this idea. I went back to my childhood, back to the one character who made me feel like I could be heroic. This character made me believe I could be educated. I could be well spoken. I could be romantic. I could fight for the people. I could stand against corruption. So I wanted to ask you, am I crazy to think that I should become the next Zorro?"

Without hesitating, Dana said, "Wilmer, you have to do this. How can I help? What do you need?"

I was almost in tears. Somebody I respected so much believed in my dream. But I steeled my voice enough to say, "Anybody can do a movie. But a movie comes out, then goes away. So I'm thinking we should do a TV series. We can create an entire Zorro universe with a longer-lasting signal. This way, we can continue to tell the story of our heritage and culture in the United States for a long time. Our new Zorro will be entertaining. He'll be a lot of fun. We need the symbol of Zorro now more than ever. He can also tell our story and who we were before this was America."

Dana put me in touch with Gary Marsh, president and chief creative officer for Disney Branded Television. I reached out to him, and he set up a meeting immediately. I pitched him the same idea. He said, "This is beautiful. The time is right. We should do this—100 percent."

Even with having the support of my two friends, the journey was only beginning. After Disney had produced the Guy Williams version of *Zorro* in the 1950s, the rights had been lost. Nobody seemed clear on how to get them back. I talked to my chief of staff,

Leo Klemm, and said, "I think we have to do this ourselves. Let's figure out who owns the rights today." We went to work, tracking down the owners. That led us to John Gertz, president and CEO of Zorro Productions, Inc., which he'd founded in 1977. He'd been responsible for the last four major Zorro movies and the last nine Zorro TV shows. We discovered that his production company holds hundreds of copyrights and more than 1,300 registered trademarks dealing with the intellectual property of Zorro.

Leo called John but got his voicemail and told him I'd like to connect. Not long afterward, Leo literally poked his head inside the room where I was in a meeting and said, "John Gertz is on the line. You need to take this." I stepped outside, phone in hand, and paced up and down Venice Boulevard.

"Mr. Gertz," I said. "You got my message. I wanted to ask you about the period English-speaking rights to Zorro."

"Yeah," he said. "Normally we don't talk about those."

"What if I told you there was an opportunity for Zorro to come back to Disney?"

He paused. "It's been sixty years. That's probably unlikely."

I told him about the meetings I'd had at Disney and how enthusiastic they were to bring Zorro back.

"Wow," he said. "That actually makes a lot of sense. The time is right, and you'd be a great new Zorro."

We hung up. I called Gary Marsh back and updated him. Gary called business affairs at Disney, and off we went. Everybody was like, "Okay, this is good; John Gertz is open to the idea. Let's figure out how to do this."

The deal took some time to ink. Almost a year went by. It was no simple matter to have Zorro return to Disney after being away that long. I waited and waited. I made phone call after phone call. I sent email after email. I never relented.

At last, one amazing afternoon, John called me and said, "Okay, Wilmer. Good news. It's official. The fate of Zorro is now in your hands."

I hung up the phone and started bawling. None of it had felt real until that phone call. For some time I just sat in my office, crying. It had taken almost thirteen years since I'd sat on my bed in Venezuela and recommitted to fulfilling that childhood dream. Now it was truly going to happen.

I dried my eyes and went back to work. A few more phone calls, and Disney sent me an offer not only to play Zorro but to executive-produce and develop the new Zorro journey for Disney.

My heart was just exploding.

Oh . . . and after all this, my agents called. They sounded a bit bewildered. "So, Wilmer, we have in our email inbox an offer from Disney for you to produce and play Zorro. You want to tell us what this is all about?"

I laughed. "Yeah, so about that. I kinda went rogue. Here's the full story . . ."

My agents were so proud and excited for me. They laughed. They cheered. They applauded my boldness. They've always been my champions. They were amazed I'd put this together on my own.

As of the writing of this book, Zorro is happening for Disney. We've announced to the press that Bryan Cogman will be our showrunner. He's known for his high level of writing on HBO's megahit *Game of Thrones*. He's truly captured the soul of Zorro. We could not be prouder to partner with him. Shortly after Gary Marsh stepped down as head of Disney Studios, he joined me as partner and executive producer of the project. Without him, I couldn't have done it. Additionally, I hope my involvement with Zorro will spawn into many other areas. A new universe for Zorro awaits. A decades-long dream of mine is being realized. The journey has already been amazing, and I pray many more good things lie ahead.

SO, ARE YOU PICKING UP THE CLUES ABOUT WHY I FEEL so compelled to debunk the word *luck*?

The superfan who talked to me in the restaurant wasn't a hater. He was at the opposite end of the spectrum. He was just congratulating me on what he considered to be my good fortune. But it's all related, and sometimes I have haters telling me that the only reason I am where I am today is because of luck.

To them, and to anyone who's waiting for luck to make something happen, I acknowledge that I've received support along the way. Sure. When thousands of unknown actors tried out for *That '70s Show*, it didn't have to be me receiving that role. It could have been somebody else. Yet when I joined their ranks in the auditions, I absolutely swung for the fences. I took a chance and created and embodied Fez, a character nobody had seen before, a character who was edgier and bolder than anybody else trying out could create. Ultimately, my take on the character won the day. That set my career in motion, and the rest was up to me. It takes hard work to create opportunities. It takes a team of agents and managers and a family who believes in you. And it also requires personal vision.

There have been so many times when I've needed to trust my vision. This concept of luck must be redefined for us all, because luck can become an excuse that people give for not trying hard enough, for not trusting their vision. Far too often, luck is something sought by the timid and the lazy. But here's the stark truth: the harder you work, the luckier you become. You create your own luck, and in doing so, more opportunities open up for you. As you journey toward the fulfillment of your dream, you will meet people who help you succeed. You will learn how to become professional. You will learn how to speak to the gatekeepers and share with them your ideas, or you learn how to side-step the gatekeepers and reach your goal by other means. Then you will put in hours, and put in more hours, and put in more hours still.

When you finally achieve your dream, or even while you're on the way, people will not attribute it to luck after they understand your fuller story. They will see where you came from. They will see what obstacles you needed to overcome. They will see how you refused to be defeated. They will realize how much it took for you to believe in yourself and your vision. They will see how you learned and grew along the way. They will be inspired at how you refused to be crushed when you heard the word *no*. Because you will have heard *no*, and heard *no*, and heard *no*, and heard *no*, and heard *no*, and heard it again and again and again. But that didn't stop you. Along the way, a project you loved fell apart. Another project you poured your heart into never saw the success it deserved. Another project was misunderstood. Another was overlooked. But you kept going. You kept fighting. You kept unapologetically and relentlessly knocking on doors. You kept dreaming. You kept moving forward. You allowed yourself to think outside the box. You became wildly creative with how you solved problems. You learned how to pitch, and you learned how to turn projects around so you showed people the value in them. You trusted your instincts, and you consistently delivered quality work, so people trusted your track record.

And now, today, you will hear someone say, "You are soooooo lucky."

To that, you will answer graciously, and you will answer with a smile on your face, even when your steak is getting cold, "Thank you, my friend. I wish luck was enough."

What you will want to say is this: "You need to know the truth about luck so you are never held back. Once you realize the truth, you will not wait anymore for luck. Instead, you will become bolder than ever before. You will become dauntless. You will be unstoppable in the quest to fulfill your own dreams. You will set one foot in front of the other and take a series of important steps so you climb your own Mount Everest. There is no such thing as luck. There is only the luck you create."

CHAPTER 14

Final Thoughts

In my mind, once more, I am back in that hospital where I'd rushed my dad during his heart attack. The doctors have just taken him back for surgery, and I know I need to trust them.

I make my way to where we will wait. All the family starts arriving. Amanda. My nephew, Christian. My sisters, Marilyn and Stephanie. My father-in-law. Friends. My mom is caring for Nakano at home. None of us know how long this day will be. I think, *No matter what happens today, at least he saw all of us kids grow up. At least he got to meet Nakano.*

We wait. And we wait. I pace. Sit. Stand. Pace some more. Sit. I'm running all the scenarios through my mind. All the promises I've made to my father. *Have I kept them all?* My biggest achievement is that he got to see me become a father. And he knows I can take care of everybody if he's gone.

I look at Marilyn, my closest friend in my growing-up years. She's doing so well these days, working as a casting director, happy and content as a person. Now that her son is older, she's been reclaiming time for herself, getting her career back. She's tearful as she waits, as we all are. But she looks more radiant than ever.

My sister Stephanie has grown up to become a beautiful, wise, and creative woman. She loves Asian culture and writes graphic novels. She's the one who helped me hone my Fez character so many years ago. She has kept her sense of humor all these years and consistently offers us all an imaginative take on life.

I'm so proud of my sisters. Who they've become. What they're passionate about. What they're doing now, and what they're going to do still in days to come.

Christian. He has turned out to be the best version of any of us. He's thoughtful, caring, selfless, kind. He'll help anybody.

Amanda. I love her with all my heart. She is the glue to our family, connecting us all. She gave me the biggest gift, making me a father.

I look around at this American family, taking in the scene. We are just one family living in the United States. United in concern. United in love.

At last we get an update. The main artery to Dad's heart has a series of clogs. He was barely getting any oxygen flow. It's serious. Very serious. He has no business being alive.

We wait some more. Another hour passes. Two. Three. Four.

At last, we receive word. Dad's out of surgery. Alive. Awake. We can each see him, but only if we go in one at a time. I feel like collapsing.

Instead, I take the elevator to the floor he's on, adjust my mask, and head for his room. His eyes are closed when I come in, and he has a lot of tubes running in and out of him.

Gently, I embrace my father, kiss his cheek, take his hand in mine. He opens his eyes. I smile at him.

"Dad," I say, "thanks for not ruining Father's Day."

It's a joke. He and I both know it. I want him to smile too. To breathe as easy as he can. One side of his mouth twitches and raises in a grin.

"*Mijo*," he whispers, barely audible. I lean closer so I can hear his faint words: "I think we have to start that diet now."

He's barely alive, but his shoulders move. Quietly, he's laughing. He wants to share this moment of levity with me. He wants me not to worry about him. Father and son. So much love. Year after year after year. Nothing but love. My eyes fill with tears. I look at my father.

For him, I laugh.

MY STORY, THE STORY OF MY FAMILY, IS NOT SO DIFFER-ent than the story of any immigrant family that comes to this country with a dream. We are a family that loves each other, loves life, loves God as best we're able, loves our new country, wants to work hard and make a better life for ourselves.

When my father recovered enough from his heart attack, he went back to work. He doesn't need to work these days for money. But he likes to work. It's what he does best, he has told me more than once. His spirit of generosity flows from him everywhere he goes, so he's chosen to work as an Uber driver in his golden years, picking up tourists at the airport and driving them to hotels and back again. A consummate extrovert, host, and guide, he loves meeting new people. The job keeps him young, he says. He brags to everybody he meets about who his son is. I can't tell you how many people have snapped selfies with my dad in his Uber and tagged me on social media.

My mother. I can say so many grateful things about my mother's sacrifices for us, her family. Mostly, I'm just happy to see her at the place she's at today in life. I remember one afternoon when we had first come to America, so many years ago now. I was walking home from the grocery store with my mom. The California sun beat down on us, hot in the sky. We were both sweating as we carried our groceries—only the bargains—and I said to my mother, "You know, one day we're going to drive."

It's almost laughable now, how simple that dream was. These days, my mother doesn't drive, but she has no problem having Christian drive her home from the grocery store with her trunk full of groceries. We don't worry about where our next dollar is going to come from so we can buy food. My mother worked hard to achieve the American dream with the rest of our family. But I realize that although we are well into our new life these days, not everybody in this country is so fortunate. That's what continues to fire me up today.

Not every immigrant child who comes to America will grow up and go to the Oscars, but that's okay; not every person wants to achieve that particular dream. The audacious spirit that flows in the hearts of dreamers is that we can come to this country and be whatever we want to be. We can dream our specific dreams and follow our individual paths. We are free to create the lives we want for ourselves, and that freedom is a big part of what gives the United States so much appeal. In this country, we are free to dream.

These days, I feel more strongly than ever that we must continue welcoming the people who don't speak English into this country. It's a humble start for many people, but I know from personal experience that not knowing English allowed me to listen to the people around me. I learned to understand the human dynamic, to feel what others feel even without words. When I didn't know English, it's like I developed this stronger sense of intuition. Somebody would want me to know or do something, and I could often sense what they wanted me to know or do even without words. It intensified my relationships. It developed my sense of empathy. I grew more curious, more compassionate, more fearless.

That boldness made me into a person of solutions, seeing the way things can be. That's why I'm an activist, not only an actor. I'm a welcoming activist, and I believe strongly that we need to stop this perpetual national argument about things where we disagree. Instead, we can each take an inventory about what we agree on. There's an important pivot we must all make. In the last few years, we Americans have been beaten over the head with a lie. We've been told we must fear each other because we are strangers. But we are not strangers, and we are all fighting for the same things at the core.

Think about our areas of agreement: we all want purpose and opportunity. We all want safety and education and security and independence. The American dream is attainable for everyone, and true leaders work to empower those around them to create an environment where good things are possible. Politics are always about human issues. Real people's lives and futures are at stake. Actual individuals. People who have families and think and breathe and hope and dream, just like the rest of us.

When will we begin to see that immigration is actually the greatest gift this country has been given? Without immigration, we wouldn't have the powerful human engine we have today. We are all immigrants in this country from some point in history. But the greatest misconception we have today is that immigrants are here to take jobs that belong to others, or that they're here only to ask for a handout. The truth is that immigrants—even if they're undocumented—provide billions and billions of dollars to the United States economy. Undocumented workers particularly contribute to the agricultural, hospitality, manufacturing, and construction industries, all necessary for helping this country thrive.

Let's look at just one country—Mexico—because it claims a lot of headlines these days. Even by conservative estimates, in 2019 alone, undocumented immigrants from Mexico earned almost $92 billion in the United States. They contributed $9.8 billion to federal, state, and local taxes. Their employers contributed an additional $11.7 billion to

Social Security and $2.8 billion to the Medicare trust fund on their behalf—money that they'll never see because they don't have the correct documentation. After taxes, Mexican undocumented immigrants spent or saved more than $82.2 billion.[1] They spent money on housing and utilities, gasoline, groceries, and consumer goods and services. They're not here just living for free. Immigrants fight our wars. They build businesses. They struggle to help build this country. We have to stop keeping people out. We have to design better systems to bring them in.

Let's look at another issue that absolutely makes me burn. United States immigration law clearly allows people who are fleeing violence and persecution in their country of origin to request asylum at or near the American border. Yet border separations between parents and their children still happen today. Regularly. Right now. This very minute.

That five-year-old clutching her teddy bear who has just been torn away from the arms of her mother and father—you don't think that little girl cries? Seriously! Does the land of the free and the home of the brave truly need this policy in place as some sort of necessary deterrent? Must we actually separate children from their parents at the border so we can stop immigrants from coming to America? Let's all take a moment to imagine ourselves in their shoes. Here is our choice: *If we stay in our country of origin, we will starve to death. If we flee to America, our daughter will get ripped from our hands. What should we choose for our family?*

It's so important that we never forget our altruism, our compassion, our humanity. Qualities such as these are what make the United States truly the dream that it is. Every person in this country bears a continued responsibility to reach out, to share and not divide, to allow and not prohibit, to collaborate through our commonalities. We start by championing the ideals we have in common. We commune where our common passions meet. We can decide to trust one another instead of believing the lie that we must fear each other. That's how we begin to bring about national healing.

Let's bridge gaps, not increase barriers. Let's put water on that flower and watch it bloom.

That's the one thing I want to leave with you now in the final pages of this book. The choice to be the United States of America—with emphasis on *united*—does take work. It does require some adjustments. It takes us all thinking not only about ourselves, about our own needs and wants, but about other people, about their needs and wants too. Those kinds of choices and that kind of work only make us stronger.

It's kinda like this. Every morning I get up and go to the gym. That requires adjustments. I'd rather stay in bed and sleep for another hour. But the gym is where confidence grows. The gym is where I better myself and strengthen myself so I can be there to help others. When I go to the gym consistently, I wake up already feeling like I'm winning the day.

We don't have to all lift the same kind of weights. Some will bench-press two hundred pounds. Others of us will walk on a treadmill. Others might swim laps in a pool. Others might simply sit in an oversized armchair and lift cans of soup. The exercise required to be a united country is not the same for everybody. We can all start wherever we are right now.

Yes, it takes resolve and understanding to work toward unity. Yet the investment is always worth it. We can continue to create a country that works well for everybody. The United States can be a land that reaches out in welcome. Ours is not a country of hate. It's a country of love, and that's what this American family is all about at our core. There is just one family in the United States: the family of humanity. We can all be united in concern. We can all be united in love. We can all be united for our own strength and good, and the strength and good of everybody.

SO THAT'S MY STORY, THE STORY OF A PERSON WITH A dream and the country that invited him in and set him on a grand adventure. It can be your story, too, because that's the true America.

Everyone is invited.

ACKNOWLEDGMENTS

I always start my toasts with the following sentence: "Very few times in life you get an opportunity to . . ." I normally follow this sentence with whatever has inspired me in that moment, and in this one, it's all of you.

If I were to acknowledge everyone who has contributed to my journey, I would have to write a whole other book, so for the sake of time, I will just say thank you to those who helped pave my road and walked beside me.

Papi y Mami, gracias por el amor y la vida que nos dieron a todos nosotros sus hijos. Su sacrificio, su valentía en traernos a los Estados Unidos, el futuro que disfrutamos, le damos gracias a Dios todos los días.

To my sisters, Marilyn and Stephanie, we've had quite a journey together, and without being together, we couldn't have gotten this far. Thank you for your love, your laughs, and unconditionally supporting me through it all. Christian, my nephew, you're next in line. You will be the best version of all of us, and in your love for your family, you're already showing us that. I'm so proud of you.

Tía Monica, gracias por las risas, por tu apoyo. Y por siempre rezar por mí, por estar a mi lado. Como yo estoy en el tuyo.

To my dream-making team at UTA led by my two sisters, Shani

and Nancy: I'm not sure you will ever understand what it means for a young immigrant kid like me to have his dreams met by people like you who have always said, "Yeah, why not you?!" And beyond that, I consider you both family. We've lifted one another through the lows and the highs, and we are still here, together.

A special thank you to my book agents, Albert Lee and Pilar Queen: You believed my story was worth telling. Your passion for literature really made me want to be a part of it, and here I am, with an actual book. I mean, who knew?

But of course the family is bigger. There's a list of dreamers and shakers who I've been proud to build with. Every single one of you has laid a brick in the foundation of who I am as a professional and as a man. Tim Phillips, Spencer Goldstein, Geoff Suddleson, Natasha Bouloki, Brittany Balbo, Matt Waldstein, Darren Boghosian, Mark Subias, Tracey Jacobs, Rene Jones, and Lizzie Thompson, I'm grateful and like Kobe said, "The job is not done."

To my managers, Jason Shapiro and Sam Maydew: you have gone along with every dream I've had and never called me crazy. Jason, proud to call you a partner and even more proud to call you my friend. Here's to the girl dad club!

Michael Gendler, thank you for teaching me to read the fine print.

To the sunshine in Sunshine Sachs, Jamie Kronfeld, Kimberly Christman, and Ally Maldonado: Thank you for listening with your heart and helping me spread the love. You are so important to me.

To the WVE crew, Maria Llambias, Don Tringali, John Pollak, Ryan Tomlinson, Jeremy Ross, Kaitlin Saltzman, Sydney Botko, Lauren Lipowski, Nico Raquel: You believe that it is not just about telling the stories and giving community voices. You believe that it's about bringing joy. Joy that should be experienced together. No matter who you are or where you come from or what you believe, in our audiences, everyone has a seat where we can all laugh and cry together. Thank you for your commitment to excellence. You're making a difference.

And to my day ones, Tadao Salima, Jessica Acevedo, and Leo Klemm: I could write a hundred pages on the many instances that made me feel grateful to have you in my life. Your trust, your loyalty, and most importantly, the love you have given me was, at times, the only thing that kept me going. I will always stand by you.

So many people have believed and given me opportunities to do what I love. In all my years as a professional storyteller, I've come across prolific, kind, and giving people who have become mentors of mine, whose personal examples of success and innovation have inspired my ambition. Bonnie and Terry Turner, Mark Brazil, Marcy Carsey, Tom Werner, Dana Walden, Shannon Ryan, George Cheeks, Kristen Graham, Mark Harmon, Gary Marsh, David Stapf, Jennifer Salke, Brian Cogman, Ayo Davis, John Gertz, Sharon Klein, Bryan Seabury, Jonathan Davis, Charlie Andrews, Robert Rodriguez, Nancy Kanter, Ted Sarandos, Dana Green, Tiffany Smith-Anoa'i, David Trainer, Joe Huff, Tom Hanks, Gary Goetzman, and Mary Vernieu. All of you had a hand in building the foundation of who I am and who I want to be.

To my USO family: thank you for inspiring me and showing me that I can also serve. Jennifer Wahlquist, "until everyone comes home." Maria Teresa Kumar, look what you've done! Jason Strauss, Noah Tepperberg, David Grutman, Mo, Purple, Brent Bolthouse, Frankie Delgado, and Frank Roberts, thank you for helping me celebrate life.

Matt Baugher at Harper Select, the next cigar is on you.

Marcus Brotherton, thank you for your guidance and helping relive the why I do it all.

Amanda and Nakano, "Everything I do, I do for you." You bring me peace, balance, and serenity, and for however long God blesses me with this life, I will enjoy every moment and love every smile. I love you both. You give me the fire to keep traveling the road, and this road wouldn't have sunshine if I didn't have you. Chimichurri, so grateful that we are on the adventure of a lifetime together. Thank God you know how to set up a tent. LOL! You remind me to pause. You remind me to appreciate every sunrise and every sunset . . . Here's to watching millions of waves break, beside you. And, Nakano, I promise you before I leave this earth, I will do everything I can to leave you a better world. Love unconditionally and believe in your heart, for it knows you better than you know yourself.

And finally to my incredible fans: I owe so much to you. For decades, you have watched me grow and have grown alongside me. Without you, art is just a blank page, a poem never read, and a song never danced to. And thanks to our shared love, we now have a book that speaks of the poetry that's been my life. This is your American story too.

NOTES

CHAPTER 5

Paul Verhoeven, dir. *Robocop*. Los Angeles, California: Orion Pictures, 1987, film.

CHAPTER 8

Ian Vásquez, Fred McMahon, Ryan Murphy, and Guillermina Sutter Schneider, *The Human Freedom Index 2021*, Cato Institute, https://www.cato.org/human-freedom-index/2021.

CHAPTER 9

George W. Bush, 2001. "Ground Zero." Transcript of speech delivered at New York City, September 11, 2001. https://georgewbush-whitehouse.archives.gov/911/response/index.html.

CHAPTER 12

Samantha Kubota, "Wilmer Valderrama on How He Feels About Criticism of Fez on 'That '70s Show,'" *Today*, September 23, 2021, https://www.today.com/popculture/tv/wilmer-valderrama-feels-criticism-fez-70s-show-rcna2199.

CHAPTER 14

"Examining the Economic Contributions of Undocumented Immigrants by Country of Origin," *New American Economy Research Fund*, March 8, 2021, https://research.newamericaneconomy.org/report/contributions-of-undocumented-immigrants-by-country/.

ABOUT THE AUTHOR

From his breakout role as Fez on the Emmy-nominated series *That '70s Show* to playing Nick Torres in the number one TV drama *NCIS* on CBS, actor, producer, and activist Wilmer Valderrama has been making audiences laugh, listen, and think for over two decades. On the big screen, he lent his voice to the Academy Award-winning Disney animated film *Encanto*, which became a cultural phenomenon. Behind the camera, in 2006, Wilmer established his production company, WV Entertainment, where he continues to develop and produce projects in the alternative and scripted spaces. Valderrama is active in several philanthropic agencies. He's the cofounder of Harness, a group dedicated to connecting communities through conversation to inspire action; serves on the board of Voto Latino; and sits on the National Hispanic Media Coalition's (NHMC) Visionary Alliance, which aims to foster opportunities for Latinx talent in the entertainment industry through the Series Scriptwriters program and the Latinx Stream Showcase. Wilmer is deeply involved with the military community, serving as a USO Global Ambassador and participating in various shows worldwide. Born in Miami and raised in Venezuela until the age of thirteen, Valderrama is fluent in Spanish and English. He and his family reside in Los Angeles.